All God's People

Archbishop Rembert G. Weakland, O.S.B.

All God's People

Catholic Identity After
The Second Vatican Council

Paulist Press † New York † Mahwah

Library of Congress
Catalog Card Number: 84-61493

ISBN: 0-8091-2665-6

Published by Paulist Press
997 Macarthur Boulevard
Mahwah, New Jersey 07430

Printed and bound in the
United States of America

Contents

III. SPIRITUALITY FOR A POST-VATICAN II CHURCH

IV. STRESS POINTS

To Father Quentin Schaut, O.S.B.,
in gratitude for introducing me to the spiritual life,
a perfect novicemaster
with a not-too-docile subject

Introduction

As I looked down through the columns I had written for the Milwaukee diocesan newspaper, *The Catholic Herald,* over the last several years, I noticed that so many of them dealt with the Church and what it means to be Catholic in this post-Vatican II era. I gathered together those articles which dealt specifically with that topic and placed them first in this book.

But there is also a host of topics which present special challenges to the Church today as it seeks its identity, and these I have placed as the second section of the book. It is not an exhaustive list, but examples of how Church life is changing in our times.

Belonging to the Church is more than just a change of attitudes about one's identity. It also implies a new emphasis on spirituality, a new way of living that faith. Perhaps one of the most striking changes has been the liturgical reform, now a part of the whole Church, and the spiritual basis of that reform. These challenges to our spirituality form the third section of the book.

But no analysis of the Church today would be complete without acknowledging that the Church has been indeed stretched to encompass new dimensions, and this, too, has produced its points of stress. In the final section of the book some of these stress points are dealt with explicitly. They involve a new relationship within the Church and between the Church and the world. They also show how old problems which were not totally laid to rest in past history rise up again when the Church seeks to redefine itself. The Second Vatican Council was the cause for resurfacing some older concerns. Just as the fathers of Vatican II, after addressing the topic of the nature of the Church, felt a need to produce a second document on the Church in our times *(Gaudium et Spes)* or a pastoral constitution on the Church as it relates to the world, so it is also necessary to face up to the existential questions posed to the Church today because of its new relationship to society. These topics will be with us for decades to come. The last section treats of those stress points.

SEEKING CATHOLIC IDENTITY IN THE CHURCH TODAY

Part I

What Does It Mean To Be a Catholic?

What does it mean to be a Catholic?

There are so many ways of answering that question, some profoundly theological, others more practical.

Since the Second Vatican Council the question has arisen in almost all circles. So many of the external practices that characterized Catholicism in the United States were dropped, and other practices, newly introduced, were not exclusive to Catholicism.

Formerly, signs of being a Catholic were such practices as not eating meat on Friday, women wearing hats in church, the confessional, the rosary and devotion to Mary. New practices introduced, such as the vernacular in the liturgy, hymn singing by all at Mass, and more Bible reading, seemed to some to be "Protestant."

In 1980, when the Bishops' Committee on the Liturgy proposed moving some holy days of obligation to Sunday, maintaining the feast but taking away the obligation of Mass attendance from others, some Catholic newspapers were full of protests. Most of them did not even discuss the question proposed; instead, they talked of the loss of Catholic identity: "one more erosion of what distinguishes us," they would say.

The problem of Catholic identity is different in the United States than in other nations. In countries like Italy or Spain the liturgical changes were accepted with very little controversy. The question of identity or its loss did not surface, because Catholicism is simply taken for granted as the only vital religion of those countries.

In the United States, on the other hand, Catholicism has always been compared to Protestantism. We may have been more especially conscious of this contrast where we felt ourselves a minority in the country fighting for our basic rights. In such a case, trying as we were to maintain our independence and preserve our faith, we put much weight on signs of identity, even if they seemed exterior and of themselves non-essential; they were emotionally very important to us. I am certain that much of that spirit still remains, even if it does not always surface in a logical way.

We are made of body and soul. We do need visible signs to hold on to, and that give us a sense of belonging to a defined group. Many feel that the ecumenical movement has blurred the dividing lines and, thus, the sense of identity. This uncertainty leaves them with a feeling of insecurity.

In the light of all of this, perhaps it would be wise to reflect, first of all, on what it means to be Christian and Catholic. One cannot do such an analysis without referring to Protestantism (we must remember how broad that concept is) and without making some comparisons; but our primary focus will be on positive, essential factors which make us who we are. Then we can look at external expressions of those beliefs and see where we are today.

And so we pose the question again: What does it mean to be a Catholic?

We shall answer that question on several levels, all of which are valid. First of all, we want to respond with an abstract answer that does not take into account differences from other Churches; second, we will take up some major differentiating characteristics of being a Catholic and how our Catholic identity affects and is affected by the ecumenical movement.

A Catholic must be a follower of Christ, one who has said "yes" to the calling or invitation which resulted in baptism. By so doing, Catholics know that they become, thus, members of Christ's body, the Church. That Church consists of people who are aware of Christ's presence among them by his word (the Bible) and his sacraments—especially the Eucharist. They believe in his mysterious presence through his Spirit in their midst, just as they are also conscious of their own personal and communal sinfulness and need for his saving grace.

A Catholic strives with other Catholics to make Christ's presence visible, as it were, in the world by acts of unselfish love and kindness in imitation of Jesus himself. Thus, they hope to be a sign to the world of God's loving care and healing power; they want to be signs of his Kingdom; they want to bring the Gospel message to others by proclaiming it in word and by witnessing to it through the quality of their lives.

Within that people of God, Catholics also are aware that some are called or designated to serve in different ways, but always in the name of Jesus and in the name of the Church. As a visible society, the Church also has a structure whose roots go back to elements implanted by Jesus in the selection of his first apostles and disciples and to the special role played by Peter among these.

Catholics recognize the Pope as the chief shepherd and supreme authority in the Church. They see that each segment of the Church has a bishop, in union with the Pope, who shares with him and the other bishops the role of teaching, sanctifying, and governing. Further, priests and deacons are called to share in various ways in that same role of service to the whole people of God.

Catholics believe that this ordained ministry is to serve the faithful so that they can grow—or that the presence of the Spirit of Jesus within them can grow—and they can share in the full mission of Jesus to transform this world.

Most Catholics live this dynamic in their lives through participation in a smaller, more neighborly faith-community or parish. It is there where they are called or gathered to receive the sacraments and the spiritual nourishment needed to face their many tasks in life. But they still have a strong sense that they belong to a larger, more universal Church and are intimately bound to all other believers in Christ.

That abstract picture becomes real when we bring into focus people we know and places we are familiar with—*our* Church. Sometimes, then, it is harder to see the whole dynamic, and we bog down at times in personality defects. We all have experienced how hard it is at times to rise above such limitations.

In this whole complex, however, what else stands out as rather distinctive to Catholics: what seems to differentiate them from other followers of Christ?

Some characteristics that could be examined are: the special unifying role of the Pope, the centrality of the Eucharist and the real presence, the special place of honor of our Lady and the saints, the sacramental system and ritual, tradition, celibacy, and religious life. On a popular plane one would also have to add "bingo."

When "outsiders" think of Catholicism, what comes first to mind? How would *they* identify us?

The first word they might use is "Papists." Without entering into the whole question of infallibility here, one can say that Catholics recognize the Pope as the foundation of unity in the Church, most especially through his teaching authority.

It does not matter how theologians split hairs on this matter, Catholics believe that the Holy Spirit abides in the Church, preserving it from error, and that the role of the Pope is central to that conviction. Catholics know that not every word of the Pope is infallible—jokes abound to prove this—but they also know that they cannot believe just anything they wish. The values of unity and continuity are high priorities in the Catholic experience, and the Pope is pivotal to both.

What may seem like intransigency and closed-mindedness in areas of faith and morals on our part is now helping all participants in ecumenical dialogue to examine more closely their own criteria for belief, since no Church holds to the theory that people can believe whatever they wish.

I have not done justice to this subject—it would take a book—but have only hinted at the emotional, and not just intellectual, response that Catholics feel toward the Pope, the living symbol and bond of universality and catholicity of the Church to them. In the ecumenical dialogue this may seem at times a hindrance, but it is also one of the important contributions that the Church makes to the dialogue with other faiths.

Yes, Catholics still have a distinctive, sometimes almost unapologetically sentimental, devotion to Mary. No Catholic would ever claim for her any graces, merits, or privileges which were not merited for her by her divine Son—even if it might seem that way to some. Today, too, we are less self-conscious of this overtly feminine and matriarchal dimension to our piety. We sense the need for models and examples of those who have been heroic in their living out of the Gospel and so dot our calendar with their memory. We hope to continue to add new ones. We intend to see a close bond between ourselves and those who have gone before us.

If you were to ask me, however, what the most significant contribution of the Catholic Church to the ecumenical dialogue today would be, I would answer: the fullness of sacramental life. How God shares his life with us humans is bound up with the way we can enter here and now into that historical moment of the death and resurrection of Jesus. Sacraments mean more than just a kind of play or drama and imply a way in which the power, the effects of a historical event transcend time and place.

Of special importance to us is the Eucharist. It is more than a horizontal sharing. As Augustine put it, we are one because we share the one body of Christ. Belief in the real presence of Christ in the Eucharist is central to understanding so much of our piety and our discipline.

Celibacy: There is no doubt that some argue there is no essential and necessary connection between priesthood, as such, and celibacy. However true that may be in the abstract, celibacy remains as a strong and important tradition in the Catholic faith. Its freeing and liberating quality should not be underestimated.

Celibacy is also a witness to the values of service to the Kingdom that takes precedence over all other concerns. It is a reminder that we do not want to fall into the error of so many in our day who equate sexual self-fulfillment with the main aim of human life.

Celibacy is an essential ingredient of religious life, another one of those "identity" marks of the Catholic tradition. Religious life flows and follows from the Gospel but acts as a witness to the whole faith-community that the needs of the Kingdom can at times make radical and all-embracing demands on some of its members.

Today the pro-life stance of the Catholic Church has become one of its identity marks. The Church in this position, as well as that on capital punishment, nuclear war, and euthanasia, is being consistent in its defense of life at all stages.

Yes, even bingo seems to be an external sign of Catholic identity. This identification certainly is not looked upon as an ideal; would that all parishes and schools were freed from this way of raising funds! It also contributes much to the negative view some have of Catholics. Bingo is, however, a symbol for a more general Catholic attitude that distinguishes us from some other religious denominations. While some, especially those who follow the Calvinistic tradition, might prohibit all use of alcohol, card-playing, and gambling, the Catholic tradition has always preached moderation in using such pleasures rather than a prohibition. Often Catholics are considered lax because of this more "Latin" tradition and also because the bounds of moderation have often been exceeded, as we all have observed.

I wish I could add humor as a distinctive quality of Catholic identity. We have to learn to laugh a bit at ourselves and accept to be fully and totally human and fallible creatures.

But Vatican II has also put demands on Catholic identity which seem new. For example, the priest faces the people today as he celebrates the Eucharist. He presides over a worshiping community; he no longer has his back to them as if leading them on a military campaign. The Scriptures have taken on new meaning in all our rites, and so the table of the word, listening to God's word, becomes essentially tied to the sacramental rite.

Perhaps, however, one of the new awarenesses in the Church which causes some confusion is the belief expressed in Vatican Council II that the Holy Spirit resides in the whole Church, in all the believers. Sometimes this belief is equated with trends which historically have led to false perceptions of the nature of the Church and which lead toward a privatization of religion—religion, that is, is viewed as being only the relationship between God and me, a private affair.

Many years ago Monsignor Ronald Knox wrote a book called *Enthusiasm,* a perceptive and classical study on aberrations in the history of the Christian tradition. In that book two attitudes are pointed out which easily distort the Christian message: (1) the emphasis on private revelation from God or the Spirit—revelation that is unmediated, direct, and in no need of legitimation by any authority outside that of the personal judgment of the recipient; (2) the emphasis on private and personal interpretation of Scripture and doctrine, living under the personal inspiration of the Spirit.

We Catholics used to label these attitudes as "Protestant," but today we find that this is not true and that they are attitudes found in all traditions, Catholic as well as Protestant. It is indeed sad that just as we are slowly overcoming such stereotypes in our ecumenical dialogue, these attitudes are again surfacing and creating divisions within our various Churches. My mail is full of literature of apparitions, usually of an apocalyptic nature, that perturb those easily frightened or easily misled. All of them seem to aim at publicity, at becoming a new Lourdes or Fatima (both of these have had legitimate approbation by the Church although never raised to the level of obligatory belief).

One finds similar phenomena or a variation on them in splinter communities—either of a very conservative nature or of the avant-garde type. Here the discernment process takes place only within a specific small community without reference to any larger ecclesial context. "What we agree on (consensus) must be of the Spirit"—they seem to say. Or, "We are the community that contains the living Spirit"— they seem to assert.

At times this temptation is found among religious as they seek new forms and ways of responding prophetically to current needs of the Church. On the other hand, the history of Christianity has shown that the charism of religious life must also be recognized by the Church and discerned in the larger ecclesial body. When St. Athanasius wrote his biography of St. Anthony of the desert, he gave to monasticism in the West—until then very suspect and prone to eccentricities—a clear approbation.

Although the monks, according to St. Benedict in his Rule, must discern who among them is to be abbot, the local bishop must come and bless the abbot, thereby recognizing the abbot's charism to be spiritual father.

Often in history we see that much misunderstanding, suffering, and trial had to ensue before this tension between the two charisms—the creative and the discerning— brought about a clear vision of the role of a particular charism in the faith-community. But that suffering was also very important in refining and honing the vision of the founder.

Today there is growing in the United States a new "Protestantizing" tendency which is more subtle, more dangerous and divisive, and which is becoming more and more rampant—flamed by several newspapers and societies. The argument runs this way: you must all be obedient and loyal to the Pope to be true Catholics; you can ignore or disobey your bishop if he is not in total agreement with the Pope. Who makes the decision as to whether the bishop or bishops are or are not in union with the Pope? The individual person or the group one adheres to does.

This attitude ignores the whole history and understanding of the relationship between Pope and bishops so clearly stated in tradition and in the documents of the Councils, especially Vatican Council II. It ignores the fact that only the Pope can declare a bishop or group of bishops no longer in union with him. It becomes a new kind of divisive ecclesiology. On the contrary, one must again affirm that the Spirit is the bond among all believers—it cannot be manipulated for personal or divisive reasons.

The Holy Spirit resides fully in all the members of the Church, and therefore the gifts of all members must come together to form the whole body of Christ. In doing so, one cannot exclude some charisms which are perhaps "uncomfortable," such as the administrative, the teaching, the hierarchical, the interpreting. A unity or consensus, when obtained by such exclusions, can only lead to greater disunity and animosity.

The unity in the Spirit between Pope and bishops, bishops and priests, clergy and laity, and among all baptized of all denominations is given by the Spirit. That unity is already present in the reality of the one baptism we all share, thus in the one Spirit. It is up to us to make that same intrinsic reality a living and functioning unity among us. It is clear: those who continually attempt to divide cannot be animated by the Spirit.

Although this phenomenon of the privatization of religion and, thus, also of the action of the Spirit can lead to the two extremes cited—one more visible on what we might call the ecclesial "left" (individual interpretation or single-community consensus), the other breaking out into a kind of new and extreme ultramontanism (a Church with a Pope and no real bishops) on the "right"—still there are many fervent and loyal Catholics who sense a loss of identity in the post-Vatican II Church.

I am not speaking here of those who yearn for "the good old days," as they remember them, where all the trying aspects have faded and the pleasant memories have been romanticized. Nor am I speaking just of those who have left the Church from indifference or lack of interest. I refer to wonderful, God-fearing people, striving to lead lives based on the Gospel and seeking to serve—people who love the Church and intend to stay in her bosom, regardless of the anguish. I am speaking of people who have accepted fully the renewal of Vatican Council II.

What is the source of such pain? Where does it stem from? These are the questions I have been asking myself.

Why are there so many lay people, in particular, who seem incapable of discussing any aspect of Church life without first having to relate all hurts and pains of a Church that seemed to or seems to neglect them?

Often the bishop becomes the personification of "Church structure," the Church as institution, and has to listen to such hurts, knowing that it is not to be taken personally. I know, however, that I become very defensive when people make sweeping generalizations about the Church bureaucracy which doesn't care, about the impersonal structure which stifles, and so on.

In spite of all our teaching to the contrary, people still identify the clergy with Church. They do not see themselves as Church. The structure is not seen as serving and ministering to the needs of all, but somewhere exists in offices far removed from the "real" needs and cares of God's people.

Most frequently such pain stems from one bad incident where an encounter with a priest left hurts and wounds. It is useless to point out that priests and bishops are human, too. The hurt is too great to see the event in perspective.

Sometimes the hurts run deeper. They come from a desire on the part of the laity—or clergy—to serve more fully, more completely; but no one listens or no one asks or no one encourages. What is frightening is that such hurts can prevent growth. They must be turned into positive moments of maturity. I would like to think that these hurts are positive signs of a greater awareness of what it means to be Church—to form a faith-community. I would like to think that these hurts are genuine signs of care and concern, and not just immature reactions.

Vatican II has also created new expectations, which have not been fulfilled. We would hope that our Catholic identity would now be seen, not so much in externals, but in our love for one another, our concern for the poor and the alienated, our lack of bigotry and bias, our sense of liturgical and personal prayer, our willingness to listen to God's Word, our eagerness to participate in the sacramental life of the Church, our promptness in listening to, receiving, and appreciating the gifts of others. These identity signs have not been realized, but the fact that we yearn for them is the best sign that our course has been correctly set. The old signs of Catholic identity need not disappear but they should be a part of this new zeal and commitment.

At this given moment in history the Catholic Church finds itself in a transition state. There is no doubt that external identity signs (like not eating meat on Friday) were dismantled too rapidly and the psychological and sociological implications were not carefully studied. People are hurting from this abandonment of traditions. Some new post-Vatican II forms have not yet solidified. Those which may seem "Protestant" (the emphasis on the Bible, for example) are really Catholic, but they are values which were neglected or placed on a second tier because of the controversies at the time of the Reformation.

Is there a fear that ecumenism may cause an erosion of those doctrines or devotions which are more specifically Catholic and not accepted by others? That fear is genuine and real, if these doctrines and values are not truly deeply embedded in our tradition. Thus far one can say that the contrary is taking place, namely, that our non-Catholic friends are looking again at the value of sacraments, of devotion to Mary, and even at the role of authority in doctrinal matters.

Is there a chance that some of the external signs of Catholic identity will return? When the bishops of the United States advised not eating meat on Friday as a penance for peace, there was such an effort to reclaim a tradition, but for a different motive. Only time will tell if this is successful. On the other hand, I was surprised to find that often the reasons for the external signs have been lost and only a sense of obligation remains without profound and justifying causes. Thus, I was surprised to see so few people in church—even those who protested my action—when I dispensed, not from the feast, but from the obligatory nature of attendance at Mass on New Year's. So many Catholics have already voted by their absence on how they perceive the nature of holy days of obligation when they occur on a workday. One must, therefore, ask the question: Is it worthwhile keeping an external sign of Catholic identity *for its own sake,* even if Catholics for the most part do not observe it? Some sociologists might say yes, but most people doubt the wisdom of such a continued practice.

The ideal must continually be striven for: solid doctrine and faith that find an adequate and convincing external sign which can rally people and give them a sense of belonging. I have observed that the post-Vatican II Church is doing just that and that the next decade will be crucial for this process.

Views of the Church

One of the most popular and influential theological books of our day has been Fr. Avery Dulles' *Models of the Church* (Doubleday, 1974). In a clear and persuasive fashion this theologian traced those models of the Church which have been evident in the Church's long history and reduced them to five principal types: the Church as Institution, as Mystical Communion, as Sacrament, as Herald, and as Servant.

Although in that same book he noted explicitly that the Church is a mystery and that there could be many more ways of looking at her and her history (he himself later added one more: the Church as Discipleship), some of his followers have been less open and have tended to restrict their vision to one or the other model. Dulles also made it clear that all these models exist simultaneously and that no one model can be absent for the fullness of the life of the Church. Dulles cautions that if the Institutional model is neglected, there will be no order and discipline. If the Mystical Communion model is absent, there will be no spiritual life. So one could go on with all the models.

I was amused recently when I received a questionnaire from someone working for an advanced degree in theology which was based on the Dulles book. I was asked which of the five models best described the Church in Milwaukee. To be true to Dulles I had to answer: All five. The author of the questionnaire had not read the cautions in the use of these models.

The Dulles models come out of a long tradition of seeing the Church as a single entity with a threefold thrust: *kerygma, koinonia,* and *diakonia.* The *kerygma* refers to the proclamation of the good news, the Gospel. That good news is, of course, Jesus Christ, his incarnation, death, and resurrection, and his sending of the Spirit. That good news must be proclaimed by the Church in word and deed. *Koinonia,* often translated fellowship or community, touches on all those elements which build up the body of Christ, the Church, and which create the new Israel, the new covenant, the new people of God. Worship and the sacramental life are at the basis of this operation of the Spirit within the Church and form its unity. *Diakonia* means service and extends the action of the Spirit to the world. It is service which keeps the Church from becoming turned in on itself, which helps it grow in love and charity. *Diakonia* keeps the Church from focusing its eyes only on the mystical and the supernatural and it helps it to become truly incarnated in the life around it.

All three of these aspects of the Church must be present at all times for it to be true to its tradition and reason for existence. To cut off any one aspect would be to deny the Church its fullness.

The Dulles models rise out of this age-old distinction and try to show the many facets, the many ways of looking at a single, complicated, and rich form of life. The Church is both of this world and not of this world; it is both natural and supernatural; it is both material and spiritual; it is both sacramental and action oriented. It has the structure and order (or hierarchy) needed for any society but it also is fellowship and service.

Reducing the Church to one model might make life easier—it would seem—but the beauty and richness of God's plan would be lost.

As rich as the analysis of the Church is which the theologian gives, whether it be that of the threefold functions just listed or that of the five models, the practical question still remains: How are all of these realized in the Church that I know and in the faith-community where I live and where I worship? In responding to that question we would kind of be theologizing from below.

The Church as Institution

No organization could long survive without a structure and a visible system of rights and duties of members, without a stable form of government which assures continuity and effective action. The Church is no exception. Jesus selected twelve apostles and gave them special powers; he placed Peter in a clear position of primacy with regard to the others. After founding new Christian communities and before leaving them, Paul had to work out a structure to carry on his work.

The model of the Church as Institution is perhaps the easiest to grasp intellectually, but it also one of the most criticized in practice. As a society the Church has to have those who govern, who can act in the name of the group, who can assure its faithful, doctrinal continuity. In addition, the Church has a sacramental system which is unique to it. For that aspect of its being it requires ordained ministers and a hierarchy. This sacramental dimension of the life of the Church makes it distinct from any other institution.

Moreover, the whole structure of the Church is focused on service, bringing the mission of Jesus to the members and to the world. The ordained ministry and the hierarchy are not places of honor, but functions to maintain the inner life of the whole group, unity of worship, and fidelity to Christ's teaching.

It is easy to see how many temptations there have been in the Church's history to let the structure become almost an end in itself instead of a means. It is also easy to see why so often people used the word "Church" to mean the hierarchy or ordained ministers rather than all of the faithful. Institution can easily become the end rather than the servant-means. Pope John XXIII, from the first homily of his pontificate to the end of his life, insisted on a self-examination on the part of the Church to maintain its role as servant.

Three temptations were pointed out in the past as being the pitfalls for the Church as Institution: clericalism, juridicism, and triumphalism.

When I returned to the United States in 1977, after spending ten years in Rome, I was surprised to find here such a strong wave of anti-clericalism. It was directed, for the most part, against bishops and those pastors who had not set up structures in their dioceses or parishes to listen to the needs and concerns of the faithful or who did not see the need to recognize the talents and gifts of the faithful and their contribution. To them it was business as usual; the pastor will make all the decisions his way. Often it was more a style of authority and a lack of sensitivity than a clearly constructed theological or ecclesiological position. The anticlericalism often had, thus, a basis for existence. People were frustrated because of a lack of a forum in which to express their discontent.

Since the Council, however, much has happened in the Church in an attempt to come to an understanding of the roles of the ordained as serving the whole body and to work out new forms of participation of all members. These steps are known to all. They have indeed been a blessing.

The question which now has to be asked is this: Are the new structures also well aware of the pitfalls of institutionalism, of clericalism? Could they easily create a new kind of lay-clericalism (if that word can exist)?

It is so easy for priest senates, diocesan pastoral councils, parish councils, liturgy committees, finance committees, education committees, directors of religious education, pastoral staffs, and so on, to become the new bureaucracy and the new form of clericalism. So often these groups are composed of people who are well-meaning and full of zeal, but not always aware of the total life of Church and especially of the spiritual and service dimensions.

Liturgy committees can make fetishes out of their own whims; finance committees can try to run Church as if profit were the name of the game; education committees can forget all but children in school; directors of religious education can set up programs for confirmation which forget that Catholic schools and parents exist. In place of the old juridicism comes a whole set of documents marked guidelines and interpreted more rigorously than any Code of Canon Law ever was. Putting a lay person in charge does not ensure a change of style or authority.

Perhaps, however, the greatest danger in the new structures is a tendency to a kind of "congregationalism" that forgets the need for the existence of the sacramental ministry and for all those structures and safeguards which the sacramental life of the Church demands.

One of the most important debates of the Second Vatican Council took place over the way to begin the document on the Church, *Lumen Gentium.* The traditional way would have been to start with a chapter on the Pope, then the bishops, then the priests, then the religious, and, finally, the laity. The first *schema* had just such an arrangement. This approach was rejected by the bishops of the world and it was decided to begin with the concept of the people of God. It was determined to outline first that the Church is one vast people, in other words, to describe the whole before looking at any of the parts.

We use the word "faithful" to characterize all the believers. Within that body of the faithful (bishops, priests, and religious are also among the faithful) there are distinct gifts and roles which come from baptism and from baptism-ordination. To diminish those distinctions would be to lose some of the richness of the body of Christ.

Ordained ministry, the document later asserts, is essentially different from baptismal, not by reason of honor or status, but because of the unique service to the Church that only those ordained can perform. Seeing in a new and more encompassing way the role of all the baptized, however, should not diminish the need for the sacramental system, spiritual leadership, pastoral training, and the like.

The purpose of the new structures is to provide a broader-based vehicle for recognizing the gifts of the Spirit in the community—the entire community—and to enable those with special gifts to contribute to the growth of the whole through their special talents. Such a concept should not do away with the need for experts, training, and education, reducing us to a Church of well-meaning amateurs.

Perhaps we are not quite there yet in providing such a structure. That may be why the new Code of Canon Law still does not mandate parish councils, unless the bishop, together with the priest senate, does so, and still describes them as consultative. (Bishops of Africa did not want them mandatory, since they feared they could be dominated in their countries by the rich and powerful and, thus, not permit the grass-roots involvement that is their main purpose.)

But parish councils are not lay organizations: they must be mirrors of the Church itself and always include clerical. They must act as a team of all ministries, baptized and ordained. They must recognize the gifts of the ordained, as well, and never develop into a "we-they" opposition. There is no such thing as a lay Church.

There must also be no dichotomy between the spiritual and the material realm. The parish council is not a group of lay financial wizards to relieve the priest of that burden so he can have more time to prepare better sermons. The material is not the realm of the lay and the spiritual that of the clergy (more about that bad dichotomy later with discussion of the other models of the Church.) Since the Church always sees itself incarnated in time and place, the material and spiritual realms will always be inextricably joined to each other.

I do not want to give here a complete course on parish councils and all the other committees which are a part of the Church today. I only wish to show that the new structures cannot just supplant old ones without also a change of attitude and perspective; otherwise, it is just business as usual under a new hat. If there is a fear of clericalism (that is, clerical domination, authoritarian methods of administration, no listening to the real needs of the faithful, no consultation with experts, no vehicles for sharing the total mission of the Church), there is also, on the other hand, the fear of "congregationalism" and the old "trusteeism." By congregationalism I mean the instruction that all are equal in every way and the Spirit is discerned by the whole group without distinctions. It reduces the clergy to a kind of hired-help, at the whim of the majority. The possible forms of politization in such a setup are evident. Trusteeism is also vivid in the historical memory of many. It implies that a group of lay people controls all the material assets. Again, a dichotomy results, one that is not a part of the Church's tradition.

Furthermore, it is a part of our Catholic identity that no local community of faith can be separated from the whole, that such a community cannot discern the action of the Spirit without belonging to and listening to a broader basis of "Church." It must listen to the Gospel together with faithful all over the world, as a part of a living tradition, and, most especially, with the Pope, and in union with all the Churches of the world and their bishops. Such a structure may seem much more complicated; but only in such a broad dynamic are we able, on the one hand, to avoid the many divisions which could result, and, on the other, to have the safeguards which will keep our tradition and following of the Gospel authentic. It is good to be C/catholic.

The question we must ask ourselves today is: How have the new forms of institution, especially those with predominantly lay participation, caught on?

Recently I compared a new brochure prepared for the 125th anniversary of a parish to the booklet that same parish produced twenty-five years earlier for its 100th jubilee. Then the parishioners prided themselves on the large number of societies in the parish, with appropriate pictures taken of all the officers together with Father Pastor. (The assistant appeared only with the youth societies.) On the 125th anniversary were reproduced pictures of the parish council, together with many, many committees. Yes, the Church had changed.

However, one cannot compare the societies with the committees, because the former encompassed a certain amount of social life with other fringe benefits for the members. The monies of the societies were often held apart from general parish funds and distributed according to the desires of the voting members—not necessarily for the visible and immediate needs of the Church. The committees, on the other hand, relate directly to parish life; but there is a minimum of social life connected with them.

Many people with whom I talk are grateful that some individuals volunteer for these councils and committees, but they themselves do not want to become involved in the tensions inherent in council and committee work. They miss, it seems, that kind of "buffer-zone" between their private life, their family, their work, and the large impersonal structures of the parish. The societies acted as that kind of "buffer-zone." Probably for this reason new societies are now emerging or old ones are being revitalized. The advantages of the societies were their more manageable size, their limited and clear spiritual demands, their possibility for sociability. RENEW and similar movements are providing some of these needs today.

I am not advocating that we regress in time to the old societies, and I certainly do not approve of societies having funds which are not controlled by the pastor and parish council—especially with regard to their disbursement. What I want, I guess, is the best of both worlds!

I could well imagine that all the eucharistic ministers of the parish would form a society, that they would develop a spirituality which would help them in their ministry (and, yes, that they would have a president, vice-president, and all the officers). Why should they not meet once a year for a diocesan congress, too?

The same could be said of the readers, the committees for liturgy, vocations, human concerns, finance, and school, the groups which minister to the elderly, the widowed, and the handicapped, and so on. All of these groups need support systems and a heightened spirituality that flows out of their ministry. These have not yet been developed, and thus "Father" must be present for every meeting. As priests become more scarce, interparochial meetings, regional congresses, and the like could help provide the incentives needed for spiritual growth.

May I add three random thoughts to clarify what was said about the Church as Institution and to avoid misunderstandings.

In the near future we will be seeing even more developments concerning Church structure on the local or parish level. Non-ordained or lay administrators are permitted by the new Code. A priest must be appointed moderator so that the sacramental life of the community can be maintained. Although I do not want to see the physical aspects of Church (the means) separated from the spiritual (what you do with them), I am not opposed to the idea of lay parish administrators—male or female. Such administrators must be faith-filled people who understand what Church is all about. They must be responsible to pastors and parish councils and to the whole Church. The priest, even though in this way freed up from so much administrative detail, does not and cannot renounce his responsibility, together with the other members of the parish council, of overseeing how the whole operation is moving along. Nor am I opposed to non-ordained men and women in pastoral roles, provided the clarity of sacramental function is maintained. (Even those who in the Church are fighting for ordination of women can see the wisdom of keeping the sacramental system very alive; otherwise, there is nothing to fight for.)

Whether the administrator is lay or priest, the role is always one of service to the needs of all. Thus, one should never use the term "monarchical" to describe the structure of the Church. Whoever is in a leadership position in Church must serve others, as the Gospel so clearly says. Moreover, there is no monarchy where all, from Pope to peon, without exception, must obey the same Gospel mandates. The Kingdom belongs to God; everyone is but an instrument of the Spirit in bringing about that Kingdom. It is the Kingdom of God we preach; it is his mandates we all obey; it is his love which must permeate our lives and our society.

We pray all together daily that *his* Kingdom come and that *his* will be done! Although new and varied structures may arise to take care of the needs of God's people, it will always be *his*—not our—Kingdom.

The Church as Mystical Communion

The second model of Church to be considered is that of the Church as Mystical Communion. As in all the models, there are so many positive and enriching aspects which come to light through an examination of this way of perceiving Church.

The term "communion" can have two different and complementary meanings here—both of them valid. It can refer to our own personal relationship to God, the "I-Thou" relationship that is indeed an essential part of religion. God created us for union with him and we know that such a union begins now. The mystics have explored for us the depths of these religious experiences. Or "communion" can also mean fellowship or mutual bonding. The basis for such bonding is grace, the life of the same Spirit in all; it is a communion of faith and love. The image which St. Paul used so often for Church as the body of Christ demonstrates the truths and beauty of this model. The gifts of the members are diversified and many, but the one Spirit animates all. Christ, who is head of the body, is the living force that permeates all: the image of vine and branches is made real.

The beauty of this model is, of course, its vitality. We had lost, in history, too much of this sense of living in unity with God and with all the members. Now we are regaining a consciousness of the need for this more spiritual dimension of Church. The role of the Holy Spirit becomes again apparent; the need for a community based on faith is emphasized; the interior or spiritual life and the role of prayer find their place among us. Since the Second Vatican Council we have been recapturing this aspect of communion *(koinonia)* and it has been enriching. Suddenly we sense a reason for the structural and institutional aspects of Church: they are to nurture, serve, reinforce, and sustain communion.

This model explains so well the Pauline concepts of charisms as gifts of the Spirit for building up the body of Christ. The unselfish aspects of God's love thus become more manifest.

Naturally, this model has also appealed to those who sense the urgency of the ecumenical movement. It permits of degrees of fellowship and relationships which strive for complete communion even when the structural aspects of such union are not yet totally clear.

I mentioned the use of the term "communion" to mean, too, the individual's immediate relationship with God. Strictly speaking, this cannot be called a model of Church. As mentioned, it is an essential aspect of religion, but cannot be a substitute for Church, because Church means people.

Nevertheless, this new awareness of the mystical, contemplative, and more personal aspect of our relationship with God cannot be lost. It is essential to Church, although not the sum total of the meaning of that word. We can be thankful then that this aspect of religion has again become emphasized in our tradition, since the modern person senses a need for such a dimension in his or her own life. Integrated with a new sense of community, this more personal or mystical religious development makes the communion model of Church so balanced and satisfying.

Are there, however, signs that this very valid and legitimate way of viewing and living Church can also be derailed or thrown out of balance? The manner of seeing Church as Mystical Communion is indeed a freeing and liberating one; but, like all freedom, it can also become a new form of rigidity and narrowness.

It is so easy to reduce religion to just an "I-Thou" relationship to God and to neglect or relegate as unimportant the social aspect of our human nature as well as the community needs which follow from it. To many people Church as a people gathered by God has no meaning. They want to exhaust or limit the religious experience of phenomenon in their lives to their own personal prayer experience. They see no point in communal worship and no relationship between religion and social change. This attitude is more prevalent in our society than one might at first imagine. It springs from our highly personalized society, where the development of the individual always seems central. One sees this attitude also in the trend toward Hinduism, Buddhism, and other

Oriental types of mysticism in which the social and communal aspects of religion do not play a dominant role.

Perhaps at the basis of most aberrations which have occurred through exaggerations of this concept of Church is the desire, the hope, the aim of having some kind of direct and immediate contact with the divine, with the Spirit. I emphasize *direct* and *immediate*. There is created then a fascination for visions and charismatic phenomena for their own sake. It is not strange that such currents become just as fascinated with direct and immediate diabolical manifestations. These two tendencies come out of the same basic exaggeration. Such a concept of Church can lead to positions antithetical to Catholic tradition—a tradition that has seen God's action in the world mediated through signs and symbols (sacraments), people, and events. Although the Church never denies God's freedom to act directly, this is not seen as the normal nor normative but as the extraordinary and infrequent.

An exaggerated concept of Mystical Communion can also lead to a type of spiritualism which we would call disincarnated, that is, without a clear identity and mission to this world. It can easily become selfish and turned in on itself. Charity and love do not become the height of Christian perfection, as St. Paul would say, but mystical and charismatic phenomena. (See his brilliant discourse in his First Letter to the Corinthians, chapters 12 to 14.) God works through his Church—and Church means living, real people. One of the demands of Church is forming community, rubbing shoulders, showing love to specific people. St. John explained this again and again in his Gospel and emphatically in his letters.

For this reason the Catholic tradition cannot be satisfied with the "electronic Church" (really a contradiction in terms, since Church means gathering of people and not isolation in individual houses). The difference is like listening to Beethoven's Fifth Symphony as contrasted with playing an instrument in the performance of the same piece.

The beauty of conceiving of the Church as Mystical Communion is its emphasis on the vertical dimension; its nemesis is that it can forget the horizontal and how the two dimensions must be integrated.

The Church as Sacrament

One of the new insights of the Second Vatican Council occurs already in the first paragraph of the document on the nature of the Church, *Lumen Gentium*. There the Church is described as a Sacrament, that is, a sign and instrument of the union which the human family possesses with God and with one another. To understand the Church as Sacrament demands a certain knowledge of one's faith and it may seem a bit abstract and theoretical. On the other hand, at the basis of this concept lies one of the pillars of Catholic identity. The word "sacrament" reveals a fundamental Catholic perception of how God relates to us and interacts with our history and how we relate to him.

First of all, God relates to us through visible realities. How could it be otherwise? We are humans. Yet he makes human objects and acts, signs and symbols, the bearers of his loving grace. Sacraments are not signs pointing to something absent, but, rather, symbolic acts signifying something present—albeit that something is invisible. The spiritual, you see, cannot of its very nature be put under a microscope or be qualitatively or quantitatively treated on graph. Yet visible symbolic acts are the conductors for divine grace. Such visible realities become mediators or bearers of something beyond our immediate perception.

Often theologians call Christ the First Sacrament, since he is the visible sign of God's self-gift of love to us. He is the "image of the invisible God," revealing the Father to us. The Church, then, his body, is Sacrament, because in its tangible, visible form it has as its aim bringing union with God and communion among people. It is a communal, or, as theologians call it, "a socially constituted" symbol.

The beauty of this way of viewing Church is that it joins the spiritual and physical in one perspective. Moreover, it respects the nature of us human persons in that we need the visible and tangible. The divine, as such, seems never within our grasp—but the sacraments are accommodations of God's goodness to our human needs and can be experienced, in faith, as human events in which his loving power is present.

Recently I noticed that this view of Church has become a part of the ecumenical dialogue. In the Introduction to the *Final Report* of the Anglican-Roman Catholic International Commission, paragraph seven states: "The Church as *koinonia* requires visible expression because it is intended to be the 'Sacrament' of God's saving work. A sacrament is both sign and instrument. The *koinonia* is a sign that God's purpose in Christ is being realized in the world by grace. It is also an instrument for the accomplishment of this purpose. . . ."

The Joint International Commission for Theological Dialogue between the Roman Catholic Church and the Orthodox Church published a document in 1982 called "The Church, the Eucharist, and the Trinity" as a first step of agreement. After a brief introduction, the very first statement reads: "Christ, Son of God incarnate, dead and risen, is the only one who has conquered sin and death. To speak, therefore, of the sacramental nature of the mystery of Christ is to bring to mind the possibility given to man, and through him, to the whole cosmos, to experience the 'new creation,' the Kingdom of God here and now through material and created realities."

As one can see, this mode of viewing Church as Sacrament is making its way into ecumenical dialogues and has been a positive contribution of the Second Vatican Council to the Church's self-understanding. It is not, however, for our day and age an easy concept to grasp and may remain more important to theologians than to average practicing Catholics.

Although there is much to recommend seeing the Church as Sacrament to the world and although this way of looking at Church has been somewhat favored by the Second Vatican Council and post-conciliar theologians, it is a bit too abstract for most Catholics. Viewing the Church as a divinely-appointed instrument for mediating God's loving grace to his people presents no difficulty as long as God's freedom to act wherever and whenever he wills is preserved. In this way the Church is rightly seen as continuing the mission of Jesus to bring God's love to all.

Probably the chief difficulty we have with this valid notion of Church as Sacrament lies in the imperfect nature of the visible Church here and now. We are not dealing with a perfect sign. By its very nature the Church, composed of fallible human creatures who are struggling, is always in pilgrimage; it is always "becoming" and never the complete image of the divine. For these reasons Pope John XXIII never ceased to remind us that the Church—you and I and all its members and structures—stands always in need of reform, renewal, and healing.

To see the Church as Sacrament or sign requires deep faith. God can use earthen vessels in their fragility as signs of the hidden mystery of God's loving self-revelation and self-giving.

Perhaps one should say that, to the onlookers, to those receiving the sign, the Church as Sacrament is more a realization of what God would want it to be and what the Church should strive to become rather than what it always, actually, externally appears to be. The Church must strive to be to the world the sign of the perfect society, mirroring Christ to the world; but we all know that we are far from reaching that goal. The Church is constantly in need of being reconciled.

A related difficulty with the concept of Church as sign or Sacrament is that we fail to see signs in our culture as effecting, that is, producing what they signify. The concept of sign in our culture is too limited to embrace the fullness of the notion of sacrament as it evolved in the Patristic period under the influence of a new-Platonic philosophy. An emphasis on the Church as Sacrament in our culture could lead to the false notion that the Church is an indicator, a sign—not the real thing. It also could lead to the erroneous way of seeing Church as "disembodied," outside the physical or real. It could seem to allow little space for historical evolution. The Church exists in time; it is not outside this world and its history.

The epitome of the sacramental nature of the Church, however, is the Eucharist. Each local Church, gathered for the Eucharist, becomes a sign—an effective symbol—of union with God, of union among the assembled members and with the universal Church. In this way it is a sign of that perfect communion, one day to be realized, with the risen Lord and all the saints.

The Church as Sacrament gives us a taste of what is to come; and so we can never confuse it with the fullness of life. The Church will thus remain Sacrament until the Lord arrives in glory.

The Church as Herald

Fr. Avery Dulles' fourth model of the Church is the Church as Herald. A new word, *kerygma,* has crept into Catholic theology in the last decades. It is now "in" to use the word "kerygmatic." Webster defines *kerygma* as "the apostolic proclamation of salvation through Jesus Christ." In the New Testament it means both the message and the act of proclaiming that message.

Salvation in the New Testament is intricately connected with hearing the word of God—not as a theological discourse, but as a herald of the good news that the Kingdom of God is at hand. It means salvation and deliverance, reconciliation and conversion, grace and truth for all peoples. Tied in with the concept of proclaiming is also the concept of listening or receiving. The Church is formed by believers, those who hear the word of God and keep it. Thus, the proclaiming of God's word becomes a salvific or saving event for those who hear it and accept it.

To many these concepts may have seemed very "Protestant" before the Second Vatican Council, but they were always part of Catholic tradition—although perhaps not emphasized in pre-Vatican II ecclesiology. Today we are fortunate in that there has been a new emphasis on the proclaimed word of God, on our response to it—especially in liturgy—and on preaching. All of this can be seen as a gain.

What are the limitations of this concept if it is not complemented by the other models?

It can lead to a literalism and an oversimplification which ignore history and the cultural presuppositions that are at the basis of all language. Yet people are attracted by its very simplicity: all one has to do is accept Jesus Christ as one's Savior. It can lead to "cheap grace."

It also leaves little room for sacraments, on the one hand, and service, on the other. Sacraments are ways of proclaiming the good news, and acts of kindness and charity are means of witnessing and preaching God's word. In the Catholic tradition the proclamation of the word, the celebration—sacramentally—of the saving events, and living out the Gospel message in life are all necessary components of Church. The temptation to limit Church to "hearing" can deprive us of the richness of our tradition.

Another weakness which ensues if this model of Church is not balanced with the others centers around the relationship between God's word and the truths about the human person, society, and nature that have been the objects of human investigation for centuries. To say that the Bible has the answers to all these questions is to fly in the face of reality. In fact, such schizophrenic thinking can only lead to irreconcilable dichotomies which produce divisions in our society that build on elitism.

One finds much of this attitude in our American religious scene today. It is the reoccurring theme of fundamentalism that preys on the anti-intellectualism of the American culture. It is easy and attractive; it gives instant security and a reason to ignore the demanding quest for reconciling new discoveries with the body of truths that went before. This tendency is not limited in its application to biblical texts and their proclamation, but finds its counterpart in the Catholic milieu with fundamentalist attitudes toward papal and conciliar texts. Such a mentality ceases to be questioning; it does not permit growth. Most of all, this exaggerated limitation of Church to proclaiming and accepting the good news in its most rigorous and literal dimension is out of keeping with the whole history of the Catholic tradition—a tradition which has alway seen the biblical vision as normative and constitutive of the Church today, but as mediated through history, events, culture, scientific, philosophical, and theological inquiry, and, especially, as guided by the presence of the living Spirit in the whole people of God.

The new gains through an awareness of the *kerygmatic* nature of the Church have indeed been many and they will continue to bring new depth to the Church of our day; but, within the Catholic tradition, they will prod us on to new inquiries, new investigations, new theologizing, and new discoveries of truth. God continues to reveal himself to us in ever-new ways. Let us not shackle his voice. At times it will be in the thunder and lightning, at times in the small whisper.

The Church as Servant

To see the Church as Servant has a certain attraction for our times. This fifth model suggested by Fr. Avery Dulles strikes a resonant tone in so many today.

One could say it began for us Catholics under Pope John XXIII with the interpretation of pastoral ministry as humble service; it flowered in the document on the Church, *Lumen Gentium,* in the Second Vatican Council; it continues to grow among us as we see the Church striving more and more to play a prophetic "servant's" role on the world scene by working for peace and justice for all peoples.

This vision of Church acts as an antidote to triumphalistic, highly-structured views or to inward-looking stances which the Church took in the past. It avoids the Marxist criticism that religion worries only about the next life and dulls people's strivings for a better life here and now.

This model has also been of ecumenical value, having been used frequently in papal documents dealing with collaboration with other Churches. All can and should join forces to work for peace and justice and in a common struggle against poverty and oppression.

The model finds its biblical roots in Luke 4, when Jesus ties in his preaching of the Kingdom with the Isaian vision of the "new" world, when the lame, the deaf, the blind will be healed and the poor will be the object of favor. It finds its model in Jesus himself and, most vividly, in his washing the feet of his disciples as a sign of the loving service they should render to one another.

The advantage of this model is certainly that it integrates striving for justice and working for charity into the whole of the Gospel message. It helps us see, as did the founders of the liturgical movement, that there is an intimate connection between altar and marketplace, between sacrament and works of love. It has also given a new sense of mission to Church and has helped it speak out to the world when Gospel values are ignored or forgotten.

Perhaps the major criticism which can be leveled against this model is that it is only a partial view and dependent on previous models. Taken exclusively, it could reduce Church to what has been called, pejoratively, the "social gospel" and neglect other aspects of living the faith. Service, or *diakonia,* has always had a broader meaning than social concerns and had included ministry to the members of the faith-community as well. The charismatic nature of the Church also includes gifts which cannot be measured by pragmatic or efficiency standards; note, for example, the contemplative orders. Unfortunately, in the United States, this model has led to a stance that avoids facing critical theological issues under the slogan: "Doctrine divides but service unites." We all have learned from experience that at a certain point in joint social efforts values must be discussed and weighed and agreed upon.

Lately I have noticed a trend in the United States (derived from vulgarizations of some documents of the

World Council of Churches) to separate Church from the Kingdom of God. Church is seen as but one of many instruments to bring about on this earth a society of peace and justice. The closer one comes to that goal the less one need talk of Church and sacraments. This view certainly does not correspond with the vision of Vatican II, which, although not identifying Church with the totality of the Kingdom, sees Church as inseparable from the Kingdom, both now and in the future. Such a new theory relativizes Church and sacraments and becomes the basis for identifying Church with social action almost exclusively. It also shifts the accent from the need for personal salvation to societal "liberation" and breaks the nexus between the two that has been so important in Catholic tradition.

Most of all, in accepting the model of Church as Servant and all its benefits, we are also reminded that the Kingdom belongs to God. Because we are but *his* servants, we need to be constantly converted to *his* ways. For this reason we must frequently hear the word and be transformed by the gift of his life-giving graces.

The following section from paragraph 39 of the document, *The Church in the Modern World,* of Vatican II should be the one which corrects our vision and keeps it from becoming too myopic or too far-sighted: "After we have obeyed the Lord, and in His Spirit nurtured on earth the values of human dignity, fellowship, and freedom, and indeed all the good fruits of our nature and enterprise, we will find them again, but freed of stain, nourished and transfigured. This will be so when Christ hands over to the Father a kingdom eternal and universal: 'a kingdom of truth and life, of holiness and grace, of justice, love, and peace.' On this earth that kingdom is already present in mystery. When the Lord returns it will be brought into full flower."

CHALLENGES FOR TODAY'S CHURCH

Part II

Each period of history has its own challenges, and the Church is not immune from such challenges and changes. It would be difficult to list all of the more engaging issues the Church must face at this moment. Certainly the question of peace comes first to mind but other questions are just as urgent. The Church has always filtered her biblical vision through contact with all truth—philosophical, scientific, theological—and has grown because of such stimulation. Today is no exception. The great influx of so many from Latin America has changed the nature of the Church in the United States and has posed a new problem of the relationship between culture and faith.

The sudden reduction in the number of priests and religious has caused a re-examination of the Church's structure and mission. The large number of older people in the Church and in society has also forced the Christian to examine the contribution that all age levels make to the life of the Church. Perhaps no area has been so full of pain and questioning as the way in which the Church should pastorally attend to the gay community, the divorced, the separated, and handle the matter of annulments.

A question which has occupied the Church in these years has been that of abortion and the value of human life at all stages. Here one senses that something has happened in our whole society with regard to our sense of sin. The whole matter of education in human sexuality has caused division in the Church and is not a subject to be discarded as unimportant.

Our age also sees a rise in the number of religious cults. This trend, as well as the number of Catholics who join fun-

43

damentalist groups, poses a whole new set of reflections for the Catholic today.

Perhaps, however, nothing has so occupied the minds and hearts of Catholics as has the nuclear threat and its dimensions. How the bishops of the United States approached this question and the whole spirit of collegiality which made such an approach possible are again new aspects of Church that have far-reaching effects for the future. This issue has indeed expanded our ecclesial sense.

In presenting reflections on these questions one knows that many others remain yet unexamined. They are but samplings of new issues or old issues seen in a new light.

The Gospel Must Be Proclaimed: Evangelization

The Gospel must be proclaimed!

As soon as possible, Jesus sent out his disciples to bring the good news to others. Mark describes that first mission experience. How excited but tired those first disciples were (Mk 6:7–13, 30–32).

We must remember that they only partially understood the good news. They did not know yet the full extent of God's love for his people; they had not yet witnessed the resurrection.

Good news meant that God was again present by his love and in his works to his people—especially to those who did not have the power or the earthly means associated in our society with freedom, advancement, and influence. The good news of God's presence could not be contained. It had to go forth from the mouths of the disciples to the four corners of the world. All had a right to hear it. Although some might reject it, the task of the disciple was to preach, not to choose which ones would decide for Christ, which ones against him. All have a right to hear God's word. We call this evangelization.

One of the most remarkable documents from the pen of Pope Paul VI is *Evangelii Nuntiandi (Evangelization in the Modern World*, December 8, 1975). After discussing the task of the Church to bring the good news to all strata of humanity and through its influence to transform from within all peoples, he treats of the relationship between Gospel and culture. The Gospel is not identical with any particular culture, he warns us, but the Kingdom of God is proclaimed to people who are profoundly linked to a culture. Evangelization is not a thin, decorative veneer, but something which penetrates to the roots. "The split between the Gospel and culture," he tells us, "is without a doubt the drama of our time." Our culture is not full of deeply religious expressions, and thus it must be regenerated by an encounter with the Gospel.

Later in the document, when he treats of the relationship between the particular Church and the universal Church, he touches again this theme. "Evangelization loses much of its force and effectiveness if it does not take into consideration the actual people to whom it is addressed, if it does not use their language, their signs and symbols, if it does not answer the questions they ask, and if it does not have an impact on their concrete life." How difficult it is to do that without betraying or twisting the essential truth and message of the Gospel! When unity of faith is maintained, this local, ethnic, cultural expression is indeed an enrichment for the whole Church.

I would like to make two pertinent observations that flow from Pope Paul's teaching.

If ethnicity is important today in the United States, it is because we often find in such cultural expressions those deep manifestations of our faith that still speak to us. American culture cannot be atheistic; nor can it be just humanistic. Our heritage is deeply religious, whether we are Irish, Polish, Italian, Latino, German, or a glorious mixture of many of these. We must listen to Pope Paul's warning about the split between Gospel and culture in our society and not create circumstances which force people recently arriving in our country to abandon their cultural expressions. In doing so, we run the risk of forcing them to lose their faith. Moreover, the contribution that such ethnic forces could make to revitalizing the religious aspects of our society would be lost. We would be the losers by suppressing their contribution.

Secondly, if we want to evangelize today, we cannot be indifferent to how we *live* the Gospel. Culture is not formed in a cerebral fashion, but is the spontaneous expression of values which are taken for granted because they are so deeply engrained in us. Every aspect of our lives must become an expression of our faith. For this reason Pope Paul calls upon us to evangelize politics, society, economics, science, art, mass media. "It also includes other realities which are open to evangelization, such as human love, the family, the education of children and adolescents, professional work, suffering."

The task he presents is indeed a challenge; but it is the Kingdom of God that is being built and God alone is the source of our strength.

Call to Priesthood

Formerly when we used the word vocation, we limited its use to vocation to priesthood and religious life. Then the word was broadened—and not without a certain logic—to include *the call to baptism and to living out that baptismal commitment in service to others.*

Today *the word often means the call to use our talents or charisms for the good of the whole community.* Sometimes it recognizes services for the faith-community which may be cultic or charitable by nature and of a more lasting quality and which are often called lay ministries. There also is a tendency to include under the word vocation many professions, especially those more service-orientated by nature, such as doctor, teacher, public official. Not everyone, however, can see life's work as so related to meaningful Christian service: work to some is only a means of sustaining life and family and not much more.

It is true, too, that there has been a negative reaction against classifying or rating callings. One can truly say that if he or she has been called to be a doctor and a parent, this is the highest calling for that individual; and it would be wrong not to answer such a calling in favor of one which might seem higher in terms of importance to the faith-community.

Nevertheless, none of these considerations should cloud the need which we have as a faith-community for those who are called to the ordained ministry of priesthood. These vocations are most needed. God calls to the priesthood whomever he wills and how he wills. This is not in our control. Although grade school children are too young to make life decisions, it is often at such an early age that the seed for a vocation is sown. How many priests can say that they were already attracted to this form of life when they were in grade school! There is also a need to foster and help discern that calling in the high school years. The boy must be left free, but, at the same time, he should not be under undue coercion to abandon such inklings. We must be supportive, but not coercive. It is the duty of the whole faith-community to foster, encourage, and pray for vocations. Of course, those who encourage most are loving and caring parents who, without undue persuasion, show their boy that they are supportive of his search and calling. Priests, too, are important models and examples and play a prime role when a young person is working out such a calling.

Perhaps all of us some few years back were too timid in suggesting a priestly vocation to a young man. Perhaps we felt that the turmoil of the times did not permit us to look favorably on giving such advice. Perhaps the large number of priests resigning from active ministry left many parents hesitant to suggest to their sons to follow such a vocation. (In passing, I might say, however, that the years of ministry of any priest who later resigned from the priesthood should not be looked upon as a tragedy but as a blessing and a gain for the faith-community.)

If in the past we were overly cautious and hesitant, could it be that we went too far in our negative estimation and now it is time to seek again a balance? We all have been hesitant to talk about vocations without also mentioning all of the other callings besides that of priesthood. There is no reason, however, not to mention the importance for the community of the priestly vocation. I would not want to minimize the many difficulties today which a young person has in accepting a calling that is for life, and especially one that involves a celibate commitment; but, surely, we should not exaggerate those difficulties nor be wanting in our faith in a provident God who also looks after those whom he calls.

Many parishioners write me that they wish we would send young priests to their parish. They should also be asking themselves what they have done in their parish to foster vocations. Have they prayed for vocations to the priesthood as a parish? Have they been supportive of those so called?

Young priests cannot be sent if they have not risen up and accepted that calling. Praying for vocations to the priesthood and being supportive of those so called is the duty of all of us.

Religious Life: Gift to the Church

In preparing a recent conference on religious life and its role in the Church, I was again struck by the perspective given to religious life in that exceptional document on the Church of Vatican Council II, *Lumen Gentium (On the Nature of the Church)*. The broad, overall outline of that document treats first of the mystery of the Church as a sign, in Christ, of communion with God and of unity among all people; it then enlarges the concept of the people of God with Christ as its head. Two chapters follow, one on the Church as hierarchical and then one on the laity.

The first outline presented to the bishops at the Council had a chapter on religious life sandwiched in between the clergy and the laity. This corresponded to an older notion that religious life was a higher state of perfection because the religious followed the counsels (poverty, chastity, and obedience) not expected of lay people, who followed only the way of the precepts or commands of the Lord.

This older model was discarded. The chapter on the laity was put first! Nor were religious described later in the light of the work they accomplish. Instead, a new optic, important for post-Vatican II development, was introduced.

After the chapter on the laity, there followed a very important chapter on "The Call to Holiness." In this chapter (number 5) it was clearly stated that all the people of God are called, each in his or her own state of life, "to the perfection of love, thus sanctifying others." Holiness is never seen, thus, as selfish, but "for others." All are equally called to holiness.

At the end of that chapter there are three paragraphs, one on celibacy, one on obedience in imitation of Christ, one on poverty. These three "counsels" are here seen as important for fostering and safeguarding Gospel values vital for the whole Church, and are not restricted to religious. Celibacy is a much needed witness to all in the Church as a sign of unselfish love and "as a singular source of spiritual fertility in the world." It is a special balance over and against so much sexual hedonism of our times and keeps all from falling into the trap of our age of seeing happiness and fulfillment only in sex. The example of Christ, who out of love "emptied himself, taking the form of a servant . . . and became obedient unto death" (Phil 2:7–8), is seen as an example for all: seeking God's will and his Kingdom comes first. The last paragraph talks of poverty and detachment from worldly things and of the dangers of adherence to riches. All our affections must be freed and directed rightly toward justice and love for all. To do this we need models and witnesses. How important those models are in our own comsumer society with its unjust distribution of earthly goods!

Finally, after the chapter on holiness, there is one on religious! It is explicitly stated that religious life is not a middle-way between clerical and lay, but is a special form of Christian life to which both lay and clerical can be called. Most of all, the charism of religious is seen as a gift of the Holy Spirit for the Church, for building up the body of Christ.

The change of optic is now clear: religious contribute to the life of the Church, not primarily by their work or apostolate, but by their very vocation. Their spirituality is

needed by all God's people. The evangelical values they foster and cherish as an essential part of their vocation is their
gift to the Church and to the spiritual life of all its members.
In this way, religious life is a sign of the hope and of the joy
which should be every Christian's; it is a sign of the living
and dying of Christ in our midst; it is a sign of a Spirit that
continues so marvelously to give gifts to the Church. Religious, through the witness of their own lives, help all members of the Church to keep their lives in perspective: God
and his Kingdom come first, they are saying to us.

Children and the Kingdom

Did you ever notice that Jesus had a special fondness
for children? All three Synoptic Gospels, i.e., Matthew,
Mark, and Luke, report in two separate instances that children were brought to Jesus or that he called them to himself
(Mt 18:1–5; Mk 9:33–37; 10:13–16; Lk 9:47–48; 18:15–
17). The oldest account of this incidence is probably in Mark
10:16. Here Jesus embraced the children and then put his
hand on their heads as a blessing. It is a shame that the later
evangelists in describing the event omit this gentle human
embrace. (They probably did not want to seem to exaggerate
the human side of Jesus too much.)

Jesus not only wanted children to come to him but he
saw in them models of his true disciples. We must ask why it
was that Jesus called attention to children as examples of
those characteristics his followers should have. Certainly he
was not sentimentally romantic about children. He knew
that they could be mischievous, often very cruel to each
other, cunning, and devious. Yet he draws attention to
them—because they are so close to the poor, the helpless,

the dependent, the defenseless whom he calls to his Kingdom. They have no power, can perform no great favors. One cultivates their love, receives it from them and bestows it on them, with no strings attached.

Yes, children are examples of the members of the Kingdom because they have nothing to give but love itself. They are not already "rich" in the goods of the Kingdom; they have nothing to return but love. This attitude must also be true of the followers of Christ, the true disciples. Membership in the Kingdom is not merited, but remains a free gift of Jesus himself. We have nothing to give but our love-filled "yes." Children are signs of the poor of the Kingdom because they have no rights—certainly that was true in Roman law—and remain so extremely vulnerable. Jesus saw himself in them because of this weakness. Children become then the most perfect image of Jesus because of his own helplessness. It is also true that children "read" people well. They seem instinctively drawn toward those who are kind and loving; they see through deception. But when they give their trust and confidence, it is full and complete and enduring. Long explanations of love seem so unnecessary.

It is, thus, quite normal that Jesus would have loved children; how could it have been otherwise? I cannot imagine anyone not loving children. In fact, I would be distrustful of those who say they dislike youngsters. I hear you saying to yourselves: "It is easy for the bishop to write all this; he doesn't have to take care of crying babies, sick babies, tired babies. He probably never had to change a diaper." You are right, but I console myself with the thought that neither did Jesus have to do those things. Perhaps for that very reason the good side, the loving side does not escape us.

There must also be aspects about our relationship to children which say something about how we pray. The same unquestioning love which characterizes our relationship with children must carry over into our prayer; we must see Jesus as being as approachable as a child. And if we, as true disciples, are also mirrored in those children, then we, too, must reach out to him and cling to him and talk to him with that same innocence and confidence and trust and love that children show us.

Has Jesus hugged you this morning yet? Placed his hand on your head? Have you hugged him?

Jethro and Exodus: The Elderly

Sometimes a lesser-known figure in the Bible can bring a very important message to God's people or be used by God as a special sign or symbol. We all know the example of Melchizedek in the Old Testament or Lazarus in the New Testament. Another interesting figure in the Old Testament is Moses' father-in-law, Jethro. (His name is also given as Reuel in Exodus 2:28.) Even though his origin is obscure and his role as a Midianite priest is not clear, his influence on Moses in chapter 18 of Exodus is remarkable. (That chapter is good reading!)

Jethro comes out to meet Moses in the desert near the mountain of God. He prays with Moses and encourages him. He also feels free to give Moses some good sound advice when he sees Moses overworking and not delegating any of his judiciary powers to those under him. It is the simple principle of subsidiarity and good management which the old man recommends.

There are two very current themes in that account which are still real for us today. The first touches on the role of the "elders" in a community, the second on delegated authority.

Jethro gives a good witness to the role of the elderly in a community. First of all, he strengthens and encourages Moses. Because of his own experience and wisdom, much respected by Moses, he is able to see God's hand in all the events which took place in the rescue of the Jewish people from Egypt. "Jethro rejoiced over all the goodness that the Lord had shown Israel in rescuing them from the hands of the Egyptians. 'Blessed be the Lord,' he said, 'who has rescued his people from the hands of Pharaoh and the Egyptians. Now I know that the Lord is a deity beyond any other'" (Ex 18:9–11).

Secondly, Jethro, because of his own experience and age, is able to free up Moses to make the kind of innovative decision necessary to adapt the role of judge which Moses was performing to the increased numbers of people and new circumstances. It was the oldster here who became the innovator! His very age and wisdom made that innovation consistent with tradition and rooted in the previous practice.

We talk much about the contribution of the elderly to our faith-community. The example of Jethro gives us a model for such participation. Jethro is a man of prayer, very aware of God's presence to Moses and his people. He is also a very positive and encouraging person. He, too, feels free to suggest a new "management" system that is innovative but a necessary adaptation.

Jethro might seem like an obscure character in that whole history of salvation, but what an attractive example for all elderly! All of the elaborate theology, too, of subsidiarity in the Church discussed at Vatican II (letting the decision be made at the lowest level possible) had been anticipated by Jethro as sheer common sense. Such a policy did not diminish Moses' role, but freed him for more important decisions and teaching. "Enlighten them in regard to the decisions and regulations, showing them how they are to live and what they are to do" (Ex 18:10)—that is the good advice Jethro gives his son-in-law.

Our Church is full of Jethros. Let them speak out: let us listen to their wisdom.

Who Is Our Neighbor?

One of the most important tasks facing us in the Church today is addressing the Gospel to various groups of people who have left the Church or who have been left out of—or denied access to—life in the Christian community. Unfortunately, as so often happens, these groups have to band together in a show of force to demand recognition. Two groups, of different nature but still needing our attention, are the divorced and gay people. Here I will deal only with the latter.

First, I would like to state that I do not have all the answers in this highly complex issue, but it seems to me that we should begin by approaching it with a sense of calm and prayerful searching, remembering the compassion that Jesus had for people who were struggling to find the Kingdom. He saw through the labels which society pinned on Gentiles, tax collectors, and prostitutes and recognized beneath these name-tags persons worth caring about simply because they, too, were sons and daughters of his heavenly Father.

Second, it is important for us to know that the bishops of the United States in a pastoral letter in 1976, called *To Live in Christ Jesus,* officially stated that homosexuality as a condition is not sinful. This realization can be of immense help to the homosexual, who thus knows that deep down there is nothing to separate him or her from God's love and care.

It is true that both in the Old and the New Testament the condemnation of acts of homosexuality is strong. Current biblical scholarship has been of tremendous help in bringing these and similar texts into a total cultural context. Homosexuality in the Old Testament was also a "national security problem" for a people constantly faced with a need for a male population sufficient to defend itself. Jesus says nothing specific about homosexuality. But St. Paul is quite explicit: he is indeed harsh with heterosexuals engaging in homosexual activity; he spoke out strongly against homosexual activity during his missionary journeys to those areas where such activity was associated with orgiastic pagan ritual sacrifices—as it had been also in Old Testament times. All these texts do exist and cannot be taken lightly, even if our knowledge of psychology and the makeup of the human person is vastly different today from St. Paul's.

Theorists are divided as to the causes of a same-sex orientation. Whether it is biological or environmental, we must accept the fact that many have sincerely tried to be "healed" of their "sickness." Experience shows that very few, even with the best therapists, are capable of changing their sexual orientation. Many are coming to the realization that God loves them as they are and that he invites them to open out in concern for others. This movement of grace cannot be ignored or discounted. Many are seeking the opportunity to grow.

Current Church teaching which we Catholics must adhere to expects gay people to remain celibate, a position which is difficult for them to accept, but, frankly, one which I cannot sidestep. Pope John Paul II, in his talk to the American bishops in Chicago, after quoting the bishops' statement that "homosexual activity . . . as distinguished from homosexual orientation, is morally wrong," then warns about holding out false hopes when confronted with such difficult moral problems. I do not take his warning to mean that such situations should not be realistically confronted nor that all hope and pastoral care are to be abandoned. I look for more dialogue among the grass-roots level, our pastoral ministers, and academic people in all fields, so that all sides can contribute to a deeper understanding of this complex moral issue.

Third, the bishops stated in that same pastoral letter: "Homosexuals, like everyone else, should not suffer from prejudice against their basic human rights. They have a right to respect, friendship, and justice. They should have an active role in the Christian community."

We have to see gay people, then, not as an enemy to be battered down, but as persons worthy of respect and friendship. Many are sincerely seeking to experience the presence of God in their lives and long to be accepted as having something to offer to the building up of the community of believers. They, too, believe in Jesus, but that does not alter their sexual orientation. In justice I would hope that we can grow beyond the myths surrounding the gay person, myths, for example, that picture all gays as perverters of children—a picture which simply is not true. We must be concerned about their rights. Consequently I cannot believe it is a Christian attitude which would block them from holding responsible positions in the community.

It seems clear to me that gay people—like all of us— fare better when they are able to develop stable relationships, when they are not relegated to a same-sex society, when they are permitted to contribute their talents to relieving injustices in our society, when they are loved and respected as people striving to grow, humanly and spiritually.

I invite all in the Catholic community to join me in showing this kind of respect as we try to work out the rightful place of these people in Church life. I ask for calm, careful study, prayer, and reflection so that we can assist all members of society in the exercise of their rights and so that no one is treated as a second-class citizen or as somehow "contaminated." Come write in the sand with me. Who is going to throw the first stone?

On Marriage and Annulments

Every Catholic, every Christian, every human being should be concerned these days about strengthening the stability of marriage in our society. The pain and suffering which follow divorce, for the couples as well as for the children, point out to us how important it is to reinforce that marriage bond.

In addition to the many programs which now are popular in any diocese, those in the parishes and those run by a diocesan office, to aid couples and whole families at all stages of growth and development, there are the many new premarital helps. Compared to just a few years ago, one can say that the Church, especially here in the United States, has been making every effort possible to help strengthen the family and family life. For those couples for whom marriage has simply not worked out, the Church now tries to provide the counseling needed to readjust. The Church wants to be involved in that very delicate and traumatic moment of separation and in the period that follows. A compassionate and realistic ministry to the divorced is absolutely necessary if we want to call ourselves a sensitive faith-community.

I feel that the Church in the whole United States can be proud of the efforts we are now making to strengthen the family by premarital programs, marriage reinforcement and peer-ministry structures, and by the more traditional marriage counseling. We also can be proud of our concern and outreach to the divorced.

The number of annulments has risen significantly in the last five or six years. In 1969 Rome gave us the American Procedural Norms which have facilitated the process for possible annulments in our American tribunals. And so, there is now a new sense of hope for divorced people to petition for annulments; in the past many of these present cases would have been backlogged.

An annulment is not a divorce and thus follows a different procedure. It simply means that the evidence gathered shows that from the beginning there was some impediment, some obstacle which would prevent the marriage from its normal sacramental growth. It never involves a question of guilt on the part of one of the parties, nor does it deny the very positive aspects of such a union that may have been present.

It is true that some theologians debate over the whole question of annulments and seek other pastoral solutions to the question of marriages that did not work out and to the possibilities of a second marriage. The Orthodox Churches, for example, do not accept divorce, but do "tolerate" a second marriage if the first did not succeed. I have no difficulty with such theological discussion, but the solutions proposed do not always seem any easier than the present one: it is a hard line to draw between maintaining the stability and perpetuity of the marriage bond and finding a compassionate and sensitive solution where the marriage has not worked out. Till any new theological discussion seems solid enough to alter traditional ecclesiastical jurisprudence, I, as a bishop, must follow the Norms laid down by Rome and universally applied throughout the world.

The Norms established by Rome for granting annulments, as well as the procedures involved, are scrupulously followed in the United States. Any assertions to the contrary are totally unfounded. I would simply advise the faithful to disregard all insinuations of what seems to be an anti-Catholic tone in some of the press. The new Code of Canon Law alters some of the procedures but does not change the basic concept of annulments nor the grounds upon which they can be granted.

I know that annulments are not well understood by the majority of the faithful; however, I have never quite understood either why people can be so nasty and uncharitable about the fact that through an annulment some are able to receive the kind of assurance they need to start life again with full participation in Church and sacramental life. Since an annulment is never granted until a civil divorce has taken place, where all the legal effects have been determined, the annulment is strictly a question of Church effects.

We all must work to reduce the number of annulments, not by arbitrarily selecting some to receive them, some not, but by cooperating in all those programs which strengthen marriage. On the other hand, we have to accept realistically that in some cases, even with all the aids and programs possible, a marriage simply has not worked out, and we must then, with compassion and sensitivity, seek ways of helping people to face life anew. Let us be mature, not narrow-minded Christians in seeking those helps and aids.

Abortion

Since abortion was legalized by the United States Supreme Court on January 22, 1973, it has become indeed the "hot" political issue of our day. It will continue to be so, since the taking of human life will always remain an issue of grave consequence. (Even those who would deny that a fetus is a "person" must admit that it is indeed a form of human life.)

It saddens me that such a large percentage of those seeking abortions are baptized in the Catholic Church. However, the percentage of Catholics seeking abortions at certain clinics in Boston and Long Island as stated in some press releases to be sixty-six percent is totally exaggerated and out of proportion; more accurate statistics usually show that the ratio is closer to the general ratio of Catholics in the United States.

Naturally, I seek reasons to explain why the Catholic conscience has not been so correctly formed on this question. Perhaps we have failed in our teaching; perhaps we have not made that teaching clear or have argued about possible exceptions so that we lost the main thrust. Vatican II's *Pastoral Constitution on the Church in the Modern World* states clearly: "From the moment of its conception, life must be guarded with greatest care, while abortions and infanticide are unspeakable crimes." I feel sure that most Catholics do indeed know the Church's teaching. Some very few may erroneously feel that whatever is permitted by law is morally permissible also for Catholics. The majority of Catholics, I feel sure, do realize the gravity of such a moral decision as abortion.

Perhaps we have not been there to help in the moment of unwanted pregnancies, supporting those who seek alternatives to abortion and helping by giving the counseling needed. Could it be that in our battle to win on a legal level we have failed to project the image of being caring, concerned people who are willing to expend our energy and our money in offering an alternative solution to those truly agonizing with such a decision? We must be a loving and forgiving, a healing and reconciling people. Few of us understand what that kind of decision, at times, must be like—pregnant, unwed or economically unsupported, and forced to face a hostile, judgmental world. Few mistakes in life carry so heavy a penalty. Most people's sins remain hidden.

Perhaps the Church seems stubborn and closed-minded in its stand on abortion to many. If it does seem unbending, it is not because it wants to be "anti" anything, but because it has such unbounded respect for life in all its forms. The Church by its nature must be truly pro-life. The respect that it has for the unborn child must also be mirrored in its respect for life at all stages. If the Church seems uncompromising, it is because it sees a connection between respect for life before birth—the most vulnerable state of all life—and respect for life at all stages, especially for the defenseless, such as the mentally retarded and the aged. The Church's recent stand against capital punishment in our own day also can be seen as a part of its general teaching that all life is a gift from God, not to be tampered with lightly by us humans for our own benefit or comfort.

To be consistent, the Church must be concerned about the quality of human life at all stages. A genuine pro-life witness includes a willingness to fight for decent housing, equal education and job opportunities, medical care, and the like, for all. Have we failed in this witness? We all rejoice at the advancements in science and technology today and the great leaps which medical knowledge has made. Surely these can be applied to protecting and sustaining life all over the globe rather than destroying it and letting it die of malnutrition and neglect. All around us today we see violence against the human person. Our hearts sicken to read in the newspapers about child abuse, sexual child molestation, rape, and all the sadistic tales which are reported there. One cannot be selective; respect for life cannot be choosy. All ages and all aspects of life are important.

We Catholics have a special reason for our respect for human life. It derives from the fact that Jesus himself took on our flesh and blood. He taught us to have respect for life and its quality. He healed the lepers and the sick, he cured the maimed. He warned us that we will ultimately be judged on how we have taken care of the physical needs of others. His whole mission, in fact, is proclaimed as a defense of the poor and the downtrodden, as being a voice for the voiceless. "Blessed are the peacemakers," he also taught us as he preached non-violence. Thus, the Church—that's you and I—must rejoice at new life, see all persons as loved by God and the objects of our concern and care.

In joining forces with all those opposed to the legalization of abortion, we should also affirm our support for the quality and dignity of human life at all stages and back those programs and groups which seek to effect a quality of life that corresponds to human dignity. Pro-life is indeed not a single issue, but implies concern for all stages of life as well as commitment and involvement in all human concerns issues.

What Happened to Sin?

Recently someone told me of an eighth word that Jesus spoke from the cross: "If I'm okay and you're okay, what am I doing hanging up here?" Although the quote is totally apocryphal, still it points out that the suffering, death, and resurrection of Christ make no sense without an awareness of sin. Redemption means nothing if we are not saved from something.

Occasionally people these days ask: What has happened to sin?

Because we beg for forgiveness of sin in the penitential rite at the beginning of each Eucharist, we are accustomed today to acknowledge often our sinfulness. Sometimes, however, this public confession of sins remains very general, without becoming explicit about our own personal sins, our responsibility for them, and a need for deep personal conversion.

What has happened to sin?

First of all, teachers and preachers sought to balance some of the negative and false concepts of God which may have been dominant in our Catholic circles with a more positive one. It was indeed necessary to present God as a loving, forgiving Father, and not as a punishing tyrant in search of offenders. God must be approachable, accessible to all. Secondly, there was an attempt to correct an exaggerated sense of guilt which was often found among Catholics— namely, that kind of guilt which resulted in a low self-image or scrupulosity and which tended to prevent a wholesome attitude toward God, one's self, and one's neighbor. There has been, thus, a conscious effort not to put people on guilt trips but to point out that the mercy of God is infinite and he waits to forgive.

Has all this done away with a concept of personal sin in our Catholic community? Hopefully not. I myself cannot imagine anyone losing an awareness of personal sin without becoming simultaneously psychologically imbalanced. Deep down—I don't care who they are—people know when they have done wrong. That voice of conscience is always there. Perhaps the younger generation if asked to come up with a list of sins according to their intrinsic evil would come up with a different ordering from that made by another previous generation, but such a difference is of degree not of substance.

We must continue to be aware of our sinfulness, our weakness as human persons, but also of our specific sins and failings. To be sensitive of conscience is not to wallow in guilt, but to be a free, responsible person. If we wish to remain free persons, then we must admit to wrong motives and wrongdoing. Knowing God is good means that we never despair but freely turn to him for forgiveness.

Yes, sin is still around—and in abundance. It will be with us forever, as long as we have free will. The battle between light and darkness is far from over and the struggle continues within us. Our entrance into Christ's death and resurrection at baptism gives us the assurance, however, that sin will not prevail. Christianity is realistic about sin, but also optimistic. God continues to love us—even in our sinfulness. "But if we acknowledge our sins, he who is just can be trusted to forgive our sins and cleanse us from every wrong. If we say, 'We have never sinned,' we make him a liar and his word finds no place in us. . . . My little ones, I am writing this to keep you from sin. But if anyone should sin, we have, in the presence of the Father, Jesus Christ, an intercessor for those of the whole world" (1 Jn 1:9–10; 2:1–2).

The Facts of Life

I confess that, although I am not a parent, I am vitally interested in the education of children and education in all its aspects, as any committed Christian should be. Here are a few principles in education to which I adhere strongly.

I know that not all ideas can be grasped in their totality at once nor at all age levels. Nevertheless, truth must remain truth, even if somehow it must be adapted to a specific age level. Simplification cannot lead to untruth.

I also know that truth is never grasped by anyone in its totality. There are so many angles to be considered; there are always new insights, and new information is always being accumulated. One will never exhaust the truths about God, the universe, the human person, and human and divine relationships. At times truth must be taught as best as possible according to our limited present knowledge and assumptions. These must be weighed for their advantages and disadvantages. Truth is more often sought with struggle than acquired by spoon-feeding.

I also know that truth is not synonymous with bare facts—although the latter are presupposed; truth belongs, too, to the realm of ideas and values. Truth is related to beauty and art and music and literature—and especially to poetry.

All of this said, in many ways I fail to understand the controversy over creationism versus evolutionism. Students today should know all scientific theories on the origin of the universe and the strengths and weaknesses of those theories—as well as what remains outside the limits of scientific proof. Faith, it is true, adds dimensions which only faith can add, namely, that nothing happens without God's intention and providential care, that the dignity of a human person and the special destiny God gives the human family make a difference in how we face life. These beliefs do not conflict with science; they simply are out of the purview of such investigation. To hide ideas or theories from students when they are able to grasp them seems short-sighted. Eventually such ideas have to be confronted. It seems much better to me to be clear, objective, and explicit in treating contrary ideas and ideologies—especially in the area of the social sciences, even if they are to be refuted and rejected.

I remember, as a senior in high school, back in 1944, that I took the complete works of Freud out of the college library. The superior found them in my study hall desk and had them "confiscated." I was told they were "dangerous." Father Maurice (I don't remember his last name), who taught college psychology, heard of this, saw me one day in the library, talked to me about Freud and his theories, and gave me a few good introductory books in psychology to read so that eventually I would be ready to understand Freud. That to me was an education!

I know that there is much discussion today on sex education. I am no expert on the amount and kind of sex education that goes with each age level. I leave that to those with more experience than I. One cannot, however, hide facts; nor can one remain on the level of generalities.

The difference between knowledge, pornography, and art should also be explained, regardless of how complicated these topics are and how thin the dividing line can be. Healthy attitudes toward the beauty of human sexuality and the relationship between sexuality and the whole of the human personality cannot be neglected.

Yes, the family should be the primary place where sex education takes place, but most parents welcome the help of those who can assist in introducing the right terminology and answer questions which are not always so clear. Most parents, too, are shy about engaging in such instruction if they have to take the initiative. I still believe the classroom is better than the alley; the classroom together with the family is best.

There is also no doubt that sexuality cannot be taught without the presentation of moral values. These values have to be a part, however, of all education and not limited to moralizing only on the matters of sex.

Perhaps the element we have neglected most in these discussions—too brief—is the person of the educator. Facts can be read in books. Ideas are but mental gymnastics if not embodied in people's lives. Values are communicated by people often more by intuition than discourse. Have we forgotten today the primary role of the educator in our society? People of faith teach science reverently—whether it be about sex or the origin of the universe. Isn't education really about "drawing out" the good, the talents, and the insights which are in people? We all are educators who are continually being educated.

Religion and the "Void"

On February 2, 1981, *The Milwaukee Journal* ran this perceptive editorial:

> *The Real Question.* Archbishop Rembert Weakland expressed concern the other day about the neofundamentalism that is affecting not only Christianity, but other world religions, such as Buddhism and Islam. We, too, are concerned—particularly about the phenomenon's potential impact on the American political process.
>
> Yet, whatever may be the dangers from a shift to the religious right, the trend poses a significant societal question. That question, which should challenge leaders and thinkers in both the religious and secular spheres, is this: What void is there in modern life that is not filled by the political philosophies and religious teachings that were once so dominant?

The question so wisely posed is a valid and challenging one. After reflecting on it for some time, I would like to express at least one personal and possible answer.

It seems to me that the "void" spoken of could be labeled "security." We live in a world that is both complex and changing. Statisticians point out how rapidly culture is changing and has changed in the last decades. There seems to be no letup in the near future. During such periods of cultural upheaval people easily become disoriented and sense profound insecurity. They look for and grasp at institutions which will be for them anchors and stable points of referral—the unchanging—to which they can hang on.

The Churches face three possible directions at moments of such challenge. The first is to create the new Church of the future, nebulous and without roots. This seldom happens, and I know of few instances today where it has been tried. For the Catholic Church, at least, it involves an intrinsic contradiction, rooted, as the Church must be, in the Gospel.

The second possibility is to change nothing and thus cater to the demands of those looking for an unchanging institution to hang on to. Each mainline Church has faced a certain division because of this tendency within it. Archbishop Marcel Lefebvre and his followers are the clearest manifestation of this tendency in the Catholic Church. Every change, even if slight, seems to threaten people in this group, as change seems like the crack in the wall that will bring the edifice down.

Even within this second category, however, one observes much inconsistency in selecting the "date" beyond which no progress can take place. The long history of the Catholic Church shows that such groups continue to survive past the period of cultural change, but never as thriving and creative forces. They remain pockets of curious, eventually folkloristic, subcultures.

The center of the road position is the one that most mainline Churches seek to adopt. It is often not the most attractive, because it must struggle with all the pain of conflict and ambiguity. It presupposes the ability to examine past positions in the light of tradition itself, differentiate between essentials and accidentals, confront new truths and new situations, and take the risk of actions and decisions which are not always clearly outlined. This latter position accepts that institutions need constant renewal, and that is painful. It avoids easy answers or just parroting previous ones. It avoids believing that all the answers to contemporary problems can be found in the Bible and seeks to answer them by a continual, prayerful understanding of the relationships which the Bible inculcates between God and the human family and among members of the human family. It sees a future to be created, but out of the values and wisdom of the past. In this regard it seeks to be realistic and admit when solutions are partial or tentative.

What happens, then, to the need for security which was the void spoken of? What does mainline religion have to say to that need?

Here I believe that the mainline Churches are true to the Bible—truer than the fundamentalists—since they place that security in God's loving providence, in his care and promise of inner guidance. That is what faith is all about.

Coupled with that faith (or, better, resulting from it) is hope—not a hope based on immobility, negation of change, or isolationism from historical reality, but one that finds its anchor in that God who, in so many marvelous ways, has looked after his people in the past and who remains with his Church today. He alone must fill that void.

Cults and Occultism

Many are asking today: What went wrong at Jonestown which led up to those mass suicides? Lacking first-hand information, one can only guess.

Perhaps it would be more profitable to examine the statement which one hears these days that such "cults" exist because the traditional religions have failed. There is a grain of truth in this assertion: traditional religion will always fail to satisfy and fulfill the fanatic fringe which occurs so often as a part of religious expression.

Excess in religious enthusiasm tends so often either to uncontrolled orgies or to fascistic conformity. The former is frequently the result when the emotion of the individual alone is the measuring rod; the latter stems from the suppression of the worth of the individual for some nebulous ideology. Both are escapes: one liberates from responsibility toward the all; the other seeks security in unquestioning obedience.

Traditional Christian religions cannot compete with excesses, because the excesses offer easy, attractive solutions; but the Gospel implies maturity and growth and a certain balance. Salvation is for the individual, but always as a part of the whole people of God with their many gifts and charisms. The gifts and charisms of the individual are for the building up of the whole. Zeal, in the Christian sense, is tempered with realism and cannot be fanaticism. It is hard for Christian enthusiasm, based as it is on a recognition of human weakness balanced by God's unfathomable love, to compete against highly emotional approaches.

Rather than scrutinize the failings of Jonestown, we would do well to look for signs of fanaticism in our own Catholic tradition. How can we recognize it? Tradition points out two areas for caution. The first is private revelation and prophecy. It is so easy to assert that one has a direct communication from God. Who can prove the contrary? Excessive eagerness for visions, prophecy and direct communication with God, especially as a means of finding answers and solutions to puzzling and vexing problems and situations, may lead to evasions from the hard realities of confrontation, searching, and suffering. For these reasons the Church has always been extremely cautious before pronouncing an opinion on the genuineness of visions and miracles. Our faith comes from the Gospel Jesus taught—a Gospel of love of God and love of neighbor. Any vision which does not lead us toward a greater unselfish love is suspect.

A second sign of fanaticism is the eagerness to find devils under every chair. Ascribing everything to the devil can also be a facile escape from facing up to our own responsibilities. The occult can be fascinating: it is mysterious, inexplicable. But history has shown that excessive preoccupation with the demonic puts the whole Gospel message out of alignment. It often indicates a warped mind that has not been touched with God's love and care. The whole victory of the resurrection becomes nullified.

Our society today tends to seek ever-new experiences, each one more stimulating than the former. Drugs, abnormal preoccupation with sex, the occult—all become attractive as sources of more stimulating experiences.

How can a Christian message of service and love, of wisdom and charity, of unselfish giving for others compete with these more enticing experiences? I am not sure I know how, but of this I am certain: Catholicism can only be true to itself, testing its own fanatical leanings, in the hope that true holiness will also have its own special attractiveness and a sober glamor.

Signs in the Skies

In times of national or world calamity my mail increases rapidly. Many ask: Is God angry at us? Is he trying to punish us?

It certainly is not easy to interpret God's mind, and we should be very hesitant to do so. We should avoid trying to exaggerate the catastrophes and to think that God is somewhere far away from us trying to punish the world. Our present situation also is unique in history. We must remember that today's wonderful means of mass communication permit all of us to be visibly present in these disturbed areas of the world through television, radio, and the press. We see disturbing and violent films which bring the catastrophe into our living room. This is new in history and makes us immediately aware of so many terrible happenings.

Many times the human race thought that the end of the world was at hand. Pope St. Gregory in the year 600 felt that such an end could not be far away because of the violence of the way in which the barbarians were overrunning the empire. The year 1000 also was a year when many thought that the end of the world was imminent. One could cite the times of plague in the Middle Ages when such an idea again came to people's minds.

Just as it is unwise to jump too hastily to the conclusion that the end of the world is near, so, too, it is unwise to fall into the temptation of seeing these catastrophes as leading up to a new kind of chiliasm or millenarianism.

Occasionally today one finds preachers talking about the events foreseen in the Book of Revelation (20:1–10). In that vision, the author sees a period of a thousand years when Christ will return to establish his earthly kingdom before the last judgment. During this period Satan will be chained. These are signs and symbols used by the author to express the power of Jesus over the devil that began with his death and resurrection and that will continue until the end of time. These years are purely symbolic to explain a whole span of history, a number which seems almost infinite.

In avoiding such literal interpretations of the Book of Revelation and being very cautious about interpreting God's mind, one should nevertheless be positive in one's search for what God wants of us at this crucial moment of history. It would indeed be foolish to think that God is punishing us; but, at the same time, one should not simply block out all of these events as if they were not happening and as if somehow God were not a part of the happenings of this world. He certainly can use such events to shake us out of our spiritual lethargy.

First of all, it is most important that we examine our lifestyle and search into our own personal selfishness. If there are enormous catastrophes, we cannot halt them tomorrow, but we can slowly begin to stem the tide of self-ishness and violence. Secondly, we must indeed increase our prayer life. When we feel so helpless and when everything seems useless, then we must be on both knees to pray. There is nothing shameful about resorting to prayer in times such as these. We, all of us, have added special intentions daily during the Eucharist for peace in the world, and those intentions must be taken quite seriously. It would be prudent for all of us to increase our attendance at Mass and to reflect more seriously and more rigorously on the demands of the Gospel way of life.

We also should be constantly aware of signs of hope. God has indeed been good to us in the past, and his goodness and fidelity will be with us at present and help us face the future. We should actively engage in those works which will bring about peace and equality. It is not just enough to sit and look at a world in turmoil. To our prayer we must add good deeds.

God is with us; but we must be aware of his presence and especially in times of disaster.

Collegiality

The word collegiality has become a popular one after Vatican Council II. Unfortunately, it has come to mean any kind of cooperative effort at any level of Church structure.

I noticed that Pope John Paul II uses the word only to refer to that unity among bishops throughout the world and prefers "shared responsibility" for the other levels of Church society. By reason of his ordination, the bishop becomes a member of the College of Bishops. The important document on the Church of Vatican Council II, *Lumen Gentium,* which Pope John Paul refers to very often as the basis of his model for Church, states that the bishops "together with their head, the Supreme Pontiff, and never apart from him, have supreme and full authority over the universal Church." Again, it states that each bishop, and that includes ordinaries and auxiliaries, has "care and solicitude for the whole Church."

The various meetings of bishops which we all must attend is a sign of that care and solicitude each bishop has to have for the whole Church. The bishop is reminded of this obligation toward the whole Church when he is ordained. I feel sure that sometimes the faithful wonder why the bishop has to be absent so often from the diocese to attend meetings for commissions and committees which deal with problems of the Church in the United States or the universal Church. I can assure you that such frequent meetings are not pleasure trips but indeed are an obligation and a way of exercising that concern for the whole Church.

The concept of collegiality derives from the unique role that each bishop enjoys in his own diocese. Paragraph 27 of *Lumen Gentium* describes the role of the bishop in his own diocese. It states that the bishops govern the particular sections of the Church assigned to them as vicars and legates of Christ. It also states that they exercise their power of governing their Church personally in the name of Christ and that this power is proper, ordinary, and immediate. It might surprise some to know that that same document says quite clearly that bishops in their own dioceses are not to be regarded as vicars of the Roman Pontiff, "for they exercise the power they possess in their own right and are called in the truest sense of the term prelates of the people whom they govern." The exercise of this power can be limited and controlled by the supreme authority of the Church, should the usefulness of the Church and the faithful require it. For this reason, the same document speaks of the special role of the Holy Spirit in sustaining each diocese and the work of its bishop.

Such phrases as stated above are indeed frightening when one considers their weight. But, thank God, the document goes on to explain how the bishop shares his ministry with the priests, and then, of course, with all.

I have been citing these texts, not to give the impression of the greatness of the bishop, but, rather, to point out the seriousness of his collegial deliberations. It is from this spirit of collegiality that the pastoral, *The Challenge of Peace: God's Promise and Our Response,* flows.

Women in the Church

No treatment of the challenges that the Church faces today would be complete without a discussion of the role of women. This can be looked at from so many points of view. One would be to examine more thoroughly so many of the studies and documents on the role of women in Church today, such documents as the report of the Special Task Force on the Role of Women in the Church in Southeast Wisconsin. Like all these studies, it was the result of many years of hearings by a most sensitive group of men and women. There one reads of so much frustration and hurt. Another approach might be theological, a study of the Bible and women and the role of women in the early Church. And another approach might be to focus on the whole question of justice and those deprived of their full potential contribution to the life of the Church and society.

There have been many articles on the above. I would prefer just a few simple remarks which to me are basic and in a sense encompass all of the others.

Our inability, reluctance, or whatever one wants to call it to use the full talents and abilities of all the members of our Church, and in this case especially those of women, means simply an impoverishment for all of us. We are depriving ourselves of so much good and so many valid complementary insights.

I always regretted that the feminine perspective was not present in the documents of liturgical renewal which we have been implementing since Vatican II. It seems evident to me that the overly rational and formal aspects of that reform would have been mollified if women also had been able to be an essential part of the discussions which surrounded that renewal. One senses the lack of this dimension, too, in the discussion and in the official documents which deal with so many medico-moral issues that involve the very being of women.

The United States, there is no doubt, is in the forefront of this issue of the role and participation of women in Church life; but one would be naive to assume that this question will not also be raised by other cultures or that it is only a U.S. phenomenon. And, even if it were, should not the Church in the United States see this as a moment when it must make a contribution to the universal Church? Yes, even Americans could claim to have the Spirit.

What is most important is that this trend be seen, not as really a problem or a question or an issue, but as a moment of growth, a moment of insight, a positive grace that leads to greater wholeness and completeness for the Church.

We can be proud to be in the forefront in working out the meaning of this action of the Spirit in our midst.

The Cain and Abel Syndrome

One of the more important paragraphs in the American bishops' pastoral letter, *The Challenge of Peace: God's Promise and Our Response,* deals with the concept of shaping a peaceful world. An important quotation from Pope Paul's encyclical, *The Development of Peoples,* summarizes the intent of that paragraph: "Peace cannot be limited to a mere absence of war, the result of an ever-precarious balance of forces. No, peace is something built up day after day, in the pursuit of an order intended by God, which implies a more perfect form of justice among men and women."

Coupled with this exhortation is a passage from Pope John Paul's World Day of Peace Message for January 1, 1983: "One must mention the tactical and deliberate lie, which misuses language, which has recourse to the most sophisticated techniques of propaganda, which deceives and distorts dialogue and incites to aggression."

These two texts say something to all of us.

Perhaps the most forceful objection which we hear to the bishops' pastoral comes from those who think that it is naive about Soviet aggression and Soviet ideology; it fails, they say, to take into account the whole underlying duplicity of communist methods; it seems to assume that we can trust the Soviets, when history has so often proven the opposite. This objection is real, but it is treated in the document. It is also an argument well known to Pope John Paul II who has spent his life dealing with such an ideology. Yet, in his January Peace Message, he still insists on the need to continue to dialogue and to avoid those progagandistic trends which stereotype nations and individuals and make all dialogue impossible.

While admitting to the historical facts of Soviet insincerity, we must avoid extending this to all Russian people so as to create a caricature of them. We can distrust the Soviet government and its expansionist desires, but we cannot imply that all Russians are deceiving people.

I recall as a boy during the second World War how many horrible things were written and said about the Germans. Then came the Japanese. I am sure we regret now the many uncalled-for nasty epithets which were used to describe the Japanese at that time. We have now forgotten those ugly phrases and continue to deal with both the Germans and Japanese in business as if those conflicts had not existed. The animosities soon change when we come more in contact with the people themselves and not just with the negotiating leaders.

It would be very un-Christian on our part to foment such racism in our day. Yes, we must love the Russians in order to be followers of Christ. We must embrace them as humans as much loved by God as we are. We must not permit ourselves to stereotype them and create a new racism in our midst.

In the extensive travels which I had to make as head of the Benedictine Order, I always cringed at the image of the "Ugly American" that I found everywhere around the globe. I always wanted to cry out that such a description did not correspond to the many Americans I knew. I considered it an injustice. But then I would return home and find just as little knowledge of the Russian people, just as many false images and stereotypes in our own papers.

We must be most cautious and avoid perpetuating the Cain and Abel syndrome in our midst. We—our generation—are truly responsible if that kind of racism continues and leads to hostility.

The Nuclear Thing

For a Christian the call to be a peacemaker is not a debatable matter. It is a Gospel mandate.

One of the tendencies of our age is to try to slip through the demands of the Sermon on the Mount with all kinds of rationalizations. We have so many reasons, we say, to think that this does not pertain to our society, since we have different social and cultural structures. But that Sermon on the Mount, and in particular the Beatitudes, will continue to haunt us, unless we are sincere and face up to the full meaning and impact of this teaching on discipleship.

So, also, in the questions which face the Church and society today about nuclear buildup or disarmament or deterrence, what divides thinking cannot, must not, be whether it is our duty to be peacemakers, but, rather, how we feel that this can be achieved in the light of the rest of the Gospel and our tradition. We must be one in our aim of seeking to find ways toward peace.

There are some today who say the way to peace is through military strength and continued more-sophisticated arms, in particular nuclear ones, and others who wish to seek continued and realistic dialogue, with ourselves taking the first steps.

Both views are fraught with dangers. These dangers come, in the first place, from the very nature of the human person prone to failings of aggressiveness as well as naiveness. Coupled with this is that aspect of the nature of the human person which is tainted by original sin and which makes any kind of solution always tinged with error and with selfishness. Power and force have indeed in the past guaranteed a sort of temporary peace, but, surely, this is not what the biblical vision tells us is what is expected of us by God. Over and over again the Bible warns us that we must guard against seeking our security in such human devices.

The Church's particular role, however, is to teach that peace comes ultimately from nothing but reconciliation. It is only in the positive seeking of unity and understanding in mutual love that true peace can occur. Reconciliation between individuals as well as between groups and larger social realities is truly the mission of the Church in the modern world. If we all are involved in peacemaking, then we all should be involved in reconciliation.

Since the work of the Church also is to prevent discords which lead to hostilities, in addition to working toward reconciliation on all levels, the Church, too, must work toward the elimination of all those aspects of our societies which lead to war. In this category, as Pope Paul VI said so eloquently, must come, first of all, the elimination of all injustices. "If you want peace, work for justice," he so clearly stated.

We can surely unite in this effort to create a just world. We can surely unite to bring about a society, a world which no longer knows the force of poverty and the lack of human rights. We can surely unite to fight sexism, racism, and all those other barriers to mutual love and support. Unfortunately, right now we are concentrating so much on the "nuclear thing" that we might neglect to work together on these others ways of achieving peace—a more lasting peace, ways also which can unite us as Christians, not divide us.

Yes, blessed are the peacemakers in the twentieth century, for they are the true followers of Christ.

Teaching and the Kingdom

During the post-Epiphany season we meditate in the liturgy on the question: Who is this child? The Gospel readings are a kind of stringing together of passages to answer that question and enlarge our own view of who Jesus was/is for us.

One of those passages is Matthew 4:23. It is one of the earliest descriptions of Jesus in action. Synthetically, Matthew summarizes what the mission of Jesus was about: "Jesus toured all of Galilee. He taught in their synagogues, proclaimed the good news of the Kingdom, and cured the people of every disease and illness." We see that three distinct works are listed: teaching, proclaiming the good news, and healing. Perhaps it may strike us as strange that teaching comes first. We probably would have been inclined to mention proclaiming the good news first. In a similar passage in Luke's Gospel (Lk 4:15), the evangelist begins the description of the first ministry of Jesus in Galilee simply with the allusion to his teaching in the synagogues.

Before going on to emphasize this mission of teaching, I would like to draw attention to the fact that Jesus does not neglect the physical needs. He heals. Later we see him moved by the crowds that seemed like sheep without a shepherd, and so he began to teach them; but he also was moved by pity because they had nothing to eat, and so he fed them (Mk 6:34–44).

Jesus is called by the name "teacher" more frequently in the Gospels than by any other title. Of course, he is a teacher unlike the rabbis of his day because he teaches with authority and does not just transmit information from the past. He does not begin his teaching with "Thus says the Lord," but with "Amen, amen, I say to you."

Unfortunately, the Gospels do not offer us lengthy teachings by Jesus. They seem so short! Often, too, they do not seem to be one logical, patterned talk but a collection of loose sayings. Yet what we do have takes us to a new revelation of God's love for us and how we must respond to that love by love of God and love of neighbor. Jesus' teaching is not highly theoretical but very practical. His most penetrating is in the parables, so striking, yet at times so elusive. Their meaning is not grasped at once.

If teaching was listed first among the tasks of Jesus in his mission, should it not be one of our primary concerns also as Church? There is a tendency among us to reduce our religion to just the healing, the physical concerns (note so many TV electronic-church programs), or just proclaiming the good news, as if that in itself is sufficient and the Spirit will take over. Jesus put teaching first. He knew that his message would require a new way of acting, a new way of responding to God and neighbor. He knew that his life and ministry had to be seen in the light of the history of God's people that went before.

It is a shame that in our day the esteem for teachers and teaching—in both the religious and the core curricula spheres—has diminished. In the Catholic tradition teaching has always been one of the important aspects of Church in its search for truth. To teach is to be like Jesus.

SPIRITUALITY FOR A POST-VATICAN II CHURCH

Part III

What Kind of Spirituality?

Changes cannot occur in the Church and its life without our own spiritual lives being affected by the shifts of emphasis. For this reason there is today a new concern about spirituality. Honesty and sincerity, two much esteemed virtues currently, become reflected in our relationship to God and to each other.

It is also true that the emphasis on Scripture and liturgy in the Vatican II documents has affected our spirituality. What may have formerly been a spirituality possible more for monks, nuns, and religious is now seen as part of the growth process in faith of all believers.

The full impact of these shifts in accent cannot be totally assessed, but gradually they will become formative of almost all Catholics. The following reflections do not intend to be complete but represent just a start at a post-Vatican II spirituality.

Integrated Spirituality

"Single-issue spirituality"—the term has not yet been invented, but perhaps it should be. It could be applied most aptly to that kind of hyperbole occasionally attached to a private devotion by its devotees or to any kind of social program without a faith-base.

An integrated spirituality must have three qualities: (1) a liturgical reference or base; (2) a personal or contemplative dimension; (3) an awareness of the needs of others, especially the poor and destitute.

Popular devotions can never take the place of liturgy. The documents of the Second Vatican Council made that point clear. The center, the apex of our spiritual life, must be the liturgy, especially the Eucharist. This same message has been repeated so often by Pope John Paul II. In the liturgy one unites one's prayer, one's offering to the Lord's. In the liturgy one hears God's word proclaimed, one is transformed by the inner life of the Lord through the working of the Holy Spirit. The liturgy re-presents in our midst the mysteries of the life of Jesus so that we can be a part of them, so that they can be the source of our life in the Spirit, so that they can challenge us and we can grow as a people.

Liturgy, however, is not a substitute for personal prayer. On the other hand, it can nurture private prayer and sustain it, keep it focused on Jesus and his mysteries. Personal prayer can also consist of many private devotions which suit our needs at a particular moment in life. But it is so important to learn to pray "on our own"—just to talk to the Lord. We are fortunate today that there are so many prayer groups which help us in this regard and show us how. The charismatic renewal has been most effective in developing this aspect of our spirituality.

But no spirituality is complete and integral if it does not lead to love of neighbor, not in just an abstract way, but also in action. It means that needs of others, too, become a part of our prayer, both liturgical and personal, and our liturgical and personal prayer makes us more sensitive to the needy.

An integrated spirituality is one, then, which has these three dimensions, not as isolated compartments, but as complementary aspects mutually sustaining and challenging each other. Liturgy should stimulate personal prayer and personal prayer should bring a new depth to participation in worship. Liturgy and personal prayer should heighten our sensitivity to social problems, challenge us, as well as give us a biblical basis for seeking solutions. Working for social justice should bring us to our knees in personal prayer and help us to see the solidarity which is ours in the liturgy as well as the vital power and love of the risen Lord in our midst.

Such an integrated spirituality never grows stale, never boxes us in, never gives in to easy, magical solutions. It permits us to be led by the Spirit and to grow.

Trinitarian Spirituality

We are fortunate to live at this time. As Catholics we have been the heirs of a spiritual legacy fostered and developed by a series of outstanding and insightful Popes since the Second World War.

I recall having had the privilege of standing in the Square of St. Peter in 1950 when Pope Pius XII declared the dogma of the Assumption. That period could be called the "Marian Age." Pope Pius reawakened a solid and theologically grounded devotion to Mary, which was later summarized by Pope Paul VI in his *Marialis Cultus* (1974) and has been continually emphasized by Pope John Paul II.

The Council suddenly made us aware again, in a dynamic way, of something we already knew theoretically: the Holy Spirit animates and empowers the entire body of Christ, the Church. We seemed to become aware again of the role and power of the Spirit in our lives and in the life of the Church. When the eucharistic prayers were translated into the vernacular, we immediately noticed—although it was there all along—the action of the Spirit which makes holy, not just the gifts, but all of us.

We owe the charismatic renewal movement a debt of gratitude for its role in making us sensitive to the action of the Spirit in our personal lives, in the lives of our communities, in the Church. The reawakening of a sense in us of being a Spirit-filled Church is a blessing.

At first, all of the research on the "historical Jesus" seemed sterile and narrow. What has happened, though, has been a yearning on the part of all to know Jesus better. The liturgical revival has also helped us center, not in an abstract way, on Jesus our brother. He had a body, too! We seem to need this point of relationship in our quest to be ourselves and still full of the divine life. People today are hungry to know Jesus better and to live closer to him. The revival in the Catholic community of interest in the Bible as a source of spirituality is but one indication. What a marvelous acquisition!

Today, too, we are moving in a new direction as we broaden our spirituality; we see over and over again that Jesus had such an intimate relationship with his Father, which he seeks to share with us. The parable of the loving Father and the prodigal son becomes the center for a new look at our own relationship to a loving God.

The outstanding exponent of this spirituality has been Pope John Paul II and especially his encyclical, *Rich in Mercy* (1980). Here he outlines the paternal and maternal characteristics of a God who loves and cares for us.

All of this brings me back to the assertion that we are fortunate to live at this time, where we have the opportunity of living in a Church which has a truly full Trinitarian spirituality. In a recent homily on St. Teresa of Avila, I noted that her spirituality was eminently "Trinitarian," since the three persons of the Trinity were not static states of being for her, but a living dynamic of life itself into which she entered fully. With Teresa as our model and guide, we, too, can enter fully into that dynamic.

A Natural Spirituality

One of the most profound insights into spiritual life can be found in writings of such medieval theologians as Thomas Aquinas in those passages where these theologians struggled with the relationship between nature and grace. Out of that tension came the realization that grace does not destroy nature, but builds upon it, and brings it to its own total fulfillment.

Thus, Pope Paul VI was reiterating an old tradition when he stated, several times, that the human is not contrary to faith, but brought to its fullest perfection *as human* through the action of grace. This theological truth affects our spiritual life as well.

Each one of us is unique. We have special gifts and talents and a combination of characteristics which make us who we are. Grace does not seek to destroy that uniqueness but to bring it to a higher purpose, to assist it to an even greater harmony by strengthening the good, holy, and positive and bringing them to fulfillment. It is true that there are some ingredients which are found in all of us because we belong to the human race, but the exact modality can alter greatly. For example, as Aristotle stated and Aquinas so often repeated, the human person is a social creature. We are not meant to live alone. For our own growth as humans we need interaction with others; we also have responsibilities toward others, toward the whole of society, which we cannot eschew. On the other hand, some people seem to be more collectivist than others. Some feel best as part of the herd; others need private space to be themselves and prefer to "hunt" alone. Psychologists have all kinds of categories into which they can place us humans—descriptive categories which are never exclusive, but only clarify personality traits without placing on them evaluative judgments of right or wrong.

Now to return to our theme. Our spiritual life must build on our own makeup. Grace is not meant to destroy who we are, but to help us to be truly ourselves. For this reason the Church has always welcomed a larged spectrum of "ways" of spiritual growth. The liturgy and the sacraments are at the basis of the need to purify and orient the collectivist instinct in all of us. The Church's long and profound tradition of meditation, silence, and contemplation, as well as its involvement in social needs, can bring out the more personalist aspects of our being. Religious orders are so many in the Church because of the many combinations and variations of the above that attract an individual who sees others with similar makeups.

Often I feel that spiritual directors try to force one into a mold in which they themselves feel comfortable, one which suits their own psychic makeup and duties in life, rather than try to understand the natural components of the person in front of them, the responsibilities each one has, and, thus, the proper balance in the spiritual dimension that would logically follow. How delicate spiritual direction can be!

The consolation which we can acquire from the profound truth that grace builds on nature for our own spiritual life is that the holier we become, the more we are developing who we are and what we are. We develop, through grace, the uniqueness of ourselves. There is no need to force people into molds or destroy those traits which make us who we are. For this reason, too, self-knowledge can lead to deeper holiness. Most of all, we should cease to lament our "combination" and simply thank God for this unique "me" whom he loves and wants to bring to fullness by sharing his life.

Have you ever watched a film where the light was bad and nothing was too clear? Suddenly, with new light, all the details begin to come through. Grace does not destroy; it simply makes it more itself and brings it to a higher end.

Spirituality for a Nuclear Age

Suddenly the Church of the United States has become aware of the risks of living under the possibility of total annihilation. As more sophisticated missiles and counter-missiles are designed and produced, as the escalating possibilities for total destruction of this planet become not just theoretical imagination but conceivable realities, more and more people are being shaken. They are asking the ultimate questions about how all this affects and should affect our way of living.

Recently I had several occasions to interreact with young people. I noticed how the nuclear threat of destruction is a reality in their lives as they grow up and try to work out their future. Recently a teacher of the Old Testament told me that the present generation of students in the seminary, quite in contrast with past generations, reads the apocalyptic literature as reality, not dreams.

The bishops, aware of this cloud which hangs over our civilization, are addressing the moral implications it raises for us. I do not want to treat that moral question which is dealt with, in my opinion, very well and very forcefully in the U.S. bishops' recent pastoral, *The Challenge of Peace: God's Promise and Our Response.* I want to center more on the spirituality which flows from this life situation. There is, you know, an intimate connection between life and spirituality!

The common spirituality of Catholics in the United States developed under the premise that we are a free nation, that we are setting our own goals and future, that we are going to protect the rights of each individual to that freedom, that these United States are, as it were, a kind of "promised land," that our ancestors came here seeking a new world which seemed limitless in its fruits and potential. For this reason our spirituality was based on industrious hard work and on the virtues which accompany it.

Certain groups in our midst, however, developed, instead, a strong spirituality which came from the opposite of freedom—slavery. The black religious spirit is an example. No one can understand the texts and poignancy of Negro spirituals without knowing the spirituality from which they came. Today many in the United States have a difficult time understanding "liberation theology" in Central and South America. It is foreign to us because it comes out of a need for emancipation and freedom. It ties in heavily to the captivity periods of the Old Testament, to the sayings of Jesus about the poor and the emarginated, to the eschatological hopes of the epistles of St. Paul.

Suddenly now we, too, in the United States find ourselves in a new situation where a threat hangs over us—a threat so great as to destroy our future. We can and must do something about it, since we are a part of the actors in the play. As that drama continues to unfold, however, we find our spirituality affected. The nuclear threat is forcing the Church in the United States to form its own "liberation theology" and spirituality, without borrowing from South America. On the other hand, it may become the bond of understanding which will begin to unite us in a common concern.

Gregory Baum recently distinguished four models of spirituality which are found in our day: the work ethic model that counts on dedication, responsibility, and self-discipline; the expansive hedonism model that works out of the consumeristic trends of our capitalistic society; the personal growth model that has been influenced by our psychological findings in recent decades; the emancipation model that one finds mostly among groups which are struggling for liberation and freedom. Baum rightly rules out the second model as an un-Christian one, but acknowledges that mixtures of the other three are indeed possible.

What is striking in our younger generation—and now, I might venture to say, in all generations—is the growth of the fourth model. The work ethic and the personal growth models depend on freedom and a concept of future that is realizable. The nuclear threat makes these models seem futile.

What are the characteristics of the emancipation spirituality that are coming into our worship and private lives?

First of all, there is again a very finite vision of the world as a delicate and fragile creation which we can easily throw into total disorder. We sense that there is a certain helplessness in the face of the future of this small planet. We sense again the destructiveness of the human family when it gets caught up in selfish and greedy ends.

Second, we find ourselves turning more easily in the midst of this realization to the good God who created and thus far sustained us and this planet. God becomes again an actor in the historical drama of our personal lives and in the life of this nation. All those texts about God alone being the source of our salvation can be read and said with deep meaning.

Third, we become more critical of pseudo-solutions which rely on human ingenuity and might rather than on God's loving mercy and power to heal us in a radical way. The horses of Pharaoh are so easily translated into our own devices of might: we see them all as empty, thrown into the sea.

Fourth, non-violence and peace become not a future to be blithely hoped for, but a personal and communal state which must be achieved here and now. I see no use in producing a document on the immorality of nuclear weapons and their use if a change of heart does not occur in each one of us that will prevent any kind of war. Non-violence and peace cannot be slogans; they must be a way of life for all of us.

Fifth, our spirituality must be derived from the Beatitudes, from the eschatological vision of Isaiah and the prophets, from the value and dignity of every person on this globe. Some will reply that this vision is communist or totally naive. It cannot be communist, since it protects the individual. It may be naive, but who knows? It has never been tried.

Sixth, we know, too, that justice and peace go hand in hand. No peaceful world exists without both. Thus, our spirituality must be one that is based on justice. That thrust cannot cease.

The Christian mission today—in a world which needs to be emancipated—must be one of bringing a spirituality of justice and peace to all peoples and all nations. There must be a new birth of the Christian message of hope and peace to a self-destroying world. No peace will ever exist until peaceful people exist. Perhaps the nuclear threat can produce in us and in those with whom we come in contact a sense that only one way to the future is open to all of us— peace. To say that there are nations or peoples on this globe who cannot understand that message is to deny God's role and his power. Our prayer has to be that he create in us new hearts, hearts of non-violence, justice, and peace, and that he help us to be witnesses to the world that all is not lost. Of course, without him there is no future. Please do not rule him out.

God and Us

God's Love Is Everlasting

How often we have heard the expression, "God writes straight with crooked lines!" We mean, of course, that his aims and designs are not always clear to us and that only with time can we begin to see the wisdom of what, at first, may have seemed to us to be capricious or even senseless.

We Americans like everything clearly planned in our lives. For example, every group today is talking about the year 2000 and planning for that new century which is coming up. We all make yearly budgets and try to project three to five years in advance. We seem to feel more comfortable in being able to look into the future even if that future seems somewhat dismal. At least, we say to ourselves, we will not be taken by surprise.

But God is a God of surprises.

The history of our relationship to God shows that he is consistently inconsistent. The Old Testament is full of surprises in that dialogue between God and his people. The unexpected so often becomes the turning point for a new beginning as well as a new insight. Luke presents a dramatic scene (Lk 4) where Jesus, using the examples of Elijah and Elisha, showed how God enlarged his concept of his people to include those not normally considered as chosen. God never permitted his people to become comfortable or complacent.

In our own personal lives this phenomenon of God's writing in crooked lines can also be frequently verified. Just when we think we have our lives all planned and figured out, God brings us to a new dimension of existence and spiritual understanding by a new and unexpected challenge. Something might happen to us, for example, that is totally unexpected—an illness, a new job, new people in our lives, new opportunities. Sometimes God's way of dealing with us is more subtle—a new insight into our motives, a new understanding of an old truth, a new way of coping with old problems.

I am sure we all have had these experiences of God's mysterious ways of intervening in our lives. Sometimes they can be upsetting. Just when we are ready to coast, we have to readjust and rethink our future. One thing is sure, however. As inconsistent and mysterious as all these moments are in our lives, and as whimsical as God may appear to us at times, God is writing straight, even if we cannot so perceive it. He is consistent in his love and in his care—of that we can be sure. His love is unchanging and everlasting.

Partners for the Kingdom

I always wondered why God just did not do everything himself. Why did he pick such clumsy partners as us humans? We seem to mess it up every time.

But that was the great risk involved in his "enfleshment," when he became one of us. His covenant with us included our share. Somehow—perhaps that is the greatest miracle—through our little efforts, he is able to accomplish his divine ends.

These thoughts were on my mind recently as I read and reread the accounts in the Gospels of the multiplication of the loaves and fishes. Six times that miracle is recorded, once each by John and Luke and twice each by Mark and Matthew. The numbers of those fed, the location, and the amount left over can vary depending on the significance of the figures for the Jewish or Gentile audience, but the basic story is always the same.

No doubt the miracle prepared the disciples for the Eucharist, since so much of the vocabulary (took bread, blessed, broke, distributed) will appear later at the Last Supper. It also brings in the messianic times of superabundance seen in a banquet, where all are satisfied and still there are leftovers. I cannot believe that any detail in the account is without some importance. In the Gospels (thank God) words and the images they evoke are never wasted!

Thus we see that Jesus does not just perform a miracle with no "props." Each time he asks what the disciples are able—on their own—to put together. He does not perform the miracle and feed the thousands *ex nihilo*. It all begins with the clearly inadequate contribution of the disciples. That bit which they put together is taken, blessed, and distributed, and it reaches beyond all expectations in feeding the crowd. That detail is but a parable of how the Kingdom will be realized in all its dimensions. We became partners of Jesus by baptism into his death and resurrection. By his becoming one of us and by permitting us to be a part of his divine life and mission, he risked the confines of human imperfection. But he also permits us to rise above that limitation. Our contribution is minimal, but absolutely necessary. He is able to bless it and somehow, as we distribute it, a superabundance results.

This thought I find consoling. We will continue in our bungling ways; but, as we go about the mission of the Church, his blessing will be there and all can be fed. Each time we participate in the eucharistic sacrifice we have the opportunity to present ourselves, our little loaves and fishes, on the altar to be transformed into nourishment for the world, food which reaches far beyond our imagination.

Close Encounters with God

Recently I read a phrase which struck me as worthy of more extended reflection: "Doubt clings to the underside of faith: uncertainty shadows trust" (Robert E. Luccock, *Preaching Through Matthew,* Nashville, 1980, p. 229).

That phrase was verified in the stories of the first appearance of the risen Lord to the disciples—appearances which we read about in the Easter season. So often there we see the doubts of the disciples, their bewilderment—even their fears. Like a candid camera, the evangelists focus on the reactions of the people, not on the event itself. Had they really encountered the risen Lord? They never recognize him immediately but only by some action (the breaking of the bread with the disciples on the way to Emmaus) or by some word and the way it is spoken ("Mary" addressed to Magdalene).

Before the crucifixion Peter had made several confessions of faith. In John 6:69 we find him saying: "We have come to believe; we are convinced that you are God's holy one." (He had just witnessed the multiplication of the loaves and fishes and the walking on the sea.) But his faith, it seemed, was yet untested. It was easier for Peter to profess his faith on the mountaintop after the transfiguration (a view of the triumphant Lord) than it was in the court of Caiaphas or Pilate when Jesus was flogged (a view of the suffering Christ).

From the experiences of Peter and the first disciples we can learn that our first encounters with God can be much different than we expect. Faith does not mean to be without doubt, but, as in the case of the disciples, to cling to the risen Lord in spite of all appearances which could deceive or discourage.

Monika Hellwig put it well when she wrote: "Some people worry when they have questions about their faith, or when they begin to realize that the old explanations, good enough before, no longer seem to offer coherent meaning. This worry is misplaced. To believe means to want to understand, and to want to understand means to be asking questions. To ask questions means to be uncertain, perhaps puzzled or perplexed" (*Understanding Catholicism*, Paulist Press, New York, 1981, p. 1). What Dr. Hellwig is saying here is an old medieval adage: *fides quaerit intellectum* (faith seeks understanding). At times we become puzzled by one or the other belief; we thought we knew what it meant and then it seems to elude us. That does not imply that we suddenly become heretical. I am sure our desire to understand what God is in our lives can remain just as profound and as sincere as it always was.

Some time ago, a test was given to elderly, devout, daily communicants in one of our major cities. They were asked to fill out a multiple choice test. One question concerned the meaning of "The Immaculate Conception." Over half circled "Virgin Birth" instead of the correct "Free from Original Sin." I am sure they continued to pray in front of the statue of the Virgin with no less devotion.

Faith means that we are open to God's revelation of himself to us, and most especially in Jesus Christ. That revelation is also limited by our human inadequacies, our imperfect concepts, our prejudices, our emotional states. Our language, too, can only imperfectly capture the divine in its fullness. Perhaps it is like looking at a magnificent piece of sculpture, which will seem enormous to us when we are little, but come more into proportion as we grow up. We cannot see it from all sides at once, and much detail will escape us at first sight. The divine revelation can never be totally caught up by us; so at times we must be content with limited vision and a stance of just awe and reverence. At times we can only say, "I believe."

God has patience with us as he continually seeks, in love, to reveal himself to us in so many ways. Do we have the same patience with ourselves? Remember that, with all the answers, there would be no room for growth. We should thus not fret over our questioning spirit. Sometimes the best solution to doubts of belief is to live a life of love and service to the fullest, and those intellectual questions will then find a proper perspective.

The Command of Love

We all recall the passage in the Gospel when the lawyer asked Jesus which commandment of the law was the greatest. Jesus answered: "You shall love the Lord your God with your whole heart, with your whole soul, and with all your mind. This is the greatest and first commandment. The second is like it: You shall love your neighbor as yourself" (Mt 22:37–39). Again, before he died, in that beautiful discourse at the Last Supper as recorded in John 15, Jesus said: "Love one another as I have loved you."

What always bothered me about these passages was the conviction that you really could not command someone to love another. Modern psychology seems to say that you cannot command someone to love, that love is not just a matter of will. You can command someone to be kind and charitable, but love goes beyond that.

Cardinal Hume, in a talk to the bishops at Collegeville, put the matter in a way which gave me new insights and dissipated my doubts. He called the command to love God and neighbor not a command in the strict sense, from outside as it were, but, rather, an explanation of the manufacturer's design. "By being a loving creature, you are being the way I made you," the Lord seems to be saying to us. In this sense, the command is from within. It means that we are truly ourselves and being as God created us to be if we are loving creatures.

In the case of love of God, this corresponds to the old catechism response to the question "Why did God make me?"—"God made me to know him and to love him and to serve him in this life and to be happy with him forever in the next."

But another problem still remains: How are love of God and love of neighbor to be two aspects of the same love? Put in another way the question could be so stated: As a human person my love is really one. How could it have objects so vastly different as God and human creatures? This question was answered for me recently as I read Karl Rahner's *Foundations of Christian Faith*. He explains that true love is not confined within the boundaries of immediate physical experience and reaches its radical Christian essence as well as its human fulfillment when it transcends those boundaries in faith and hope. Such a love can be directed thus, he tells us, to Jesus. This following dense paragraph is worthy of a long meditation: "A person can love (Jesus) as a true man in the most proper and vital meaning of this word. Indeed, because of who the God-man is, this love is even the absolute instance of a love in which love for a man and love for God find their most radical unity and mediate each other mutually. Jesus is the most concrete absolute, and therefore it is in love for him that love reaches the most absolute concreteness and absence of ambiguity which it seeks by its very nature. For love is not a movement towards an abstract ideal, but towards concrete, individual and irreducible uniqueness, and this very love finds in its Thou the absolute expanse of incomprehensible mystery" (p. 310).

I have many more problems about love of God and its relationship to love of neighbor, but reflections on these presented will hold me for a while.

God and the Ordinary

One of my favorite stories in the Old Testament can be found in 2 Kings 5. It takes place in the time of Jehoram, king of Israel (849–842). A Jewish girl was taken captive by the Arameans and made the servant of the wife of the commander Naaman, the leper. The girl convinced her mistress that Naaman would be cured of his leprosy if he went to the prophet Elisha in Samaria. After some persuasion, Naaman did just that. The interesting scene occurs when Elisha sends Naaman the message that he will be healed if he washes seven times in the Jordan River. Naaman is angry, having expected the prophet to come out to cure the leprosy by moving his hand over the leprous spot and muttering some sort of incantation. "Are not the rivers of Damascus better than the waters of Israel? Why couldn't I wash in them and be cleansed?" asks Naaman with a certain logic. He is angry and ready to go home, when his servants convince him otherwise by arguing that if the prophet had asked him to do something extraordinary he would have done it. So, they say, why not try this simple, ordinary act? Naaman gives in, and, after washing seven times, is cured.

There is a part of Naaman in all of us! We want God to act in our lives only in extraordinary, miraculous, striking ways. Fortunately for us, that is not the way it is. We also want God to act directly; we want no intermediaries. But, again, that is, for the most part, not the way it is. God uses the ordinary objects and actions of our lives.

This story of Naaman, it seems to me, helps us in a very special way to understand what the sacraments are about. We remember the catechism definition: A sacrament is an outward sign instituted by Christ to give grace. Sacraments are ordinary signs, like washing with water (baptism) and eating bread and drinking wine (Eucharist). These signs are within the reach of all; they are a part of ordinary life and are easily understood. The medieval adage, often repeated, states: *Sacramenta propter homines*—Sacraments are for people. God, in a beautiful and simple way, comes down to our size, our mentality, our sensibilities. God has truly been good to us. Sometimes, like Naaman, we have to be persuaded that God's way is best. We can become too sophisticated, too intellectual, and try to project onto God how we think he should act among us. If he were to ask the heroic and unusual of us, we would—we think—find it easier to believe.

But God is not contained by our fancies and instead shows us how the ordinary can be made extraordinary. His healing presence is not to be tied or bound to the extraordinary or to that which would be the prerogative of but a few. Water, oil, bread, wine—these are the elemental objects and vehicles for his saving acts. It took the uneducated and believing servants to convince the commander Naaman that God would use even the muddy Jordan to heal and cleanse. Hopefully we will see, too, without too much persuasion, that God can act in our lives through ordinary objects and events and especially through the sacraments.

Growth in Faith

Have you noticed the various stages people go through after they buy a Rubik Cube? First, they try endlessly to work it out and succeed usually as far as solving one side. Then they buy an instruction book and, with patience, learn how to follow the moves. The third stage is an attempt to memorize the moves so they can do it without the book. (At this stage many fall by the wayside.) Finally comes the stage of *understanding* what moves produce what desired effects. Once that stage arrives, new creative possibilities open up and it all begins to make sense.

I was thinking of this recently as a kind of image of what happens in our religious life. It is not an adequate image—for a reason I will point out later—but it made one good point. So many times we had to learn things that we did not understand. We had to memorize formulas or prayers. What is a sacrament? What is inspiration of the Bible all about? What is the good news? What is penance? Why go to Mass on Sunday? As we grow older, we have all kinds of questions and doubts. That is only natural. We have to check out those formulas and pat answers against our own inner feelings and with life's experiences. Faith involves a long process, since we have to appropriate slowly all of what we learn to ourselves in an ever-new way. Every bit of conviction involves a new beginning. Just when we think we have it all together (like the Rubik Cube), we goof and feel we are starting over.

There are two ways, however, in which my image fails. The first aspect—not covered in this example—is that faith involves a personal relationship to God and not just to a body of beliefs. God is a person, not a puzzle. Like all persons, he is also a beautiful mystery. How long it takes us humans to get to know each other! How much more complicated to us is knowing God and how he reveals himself—in love—to us! All relationships take time. That is true with our family, with our friends, with our teachers. Why not with God? Here is where prayer comes in. To know someone, we have to spend time with that person and exchange experiences, hopes, disappointments. God will never be a person to me if I do not take time to be with him.

Another important aspect of our faith that is not found in the Rubik Cube example is that God also has revealed to us who he is through other people and events. Our search for him and his ways is not done alone. He entered human history to be one of us and is with us as he makes us into his people. For this reason, religion is not just a personal matter. He is Father to us all; Jesus is Brother to us all. Sometimes belonging to a faith-community seems to complicate life, but ultimately it makes it fuller and richer. We know we are never alone in seeking God; we know we are supported by many others. In turn, we must also look out to others, in order to support and sustain them. God wants us to find him in those relationships.

Life is a lot more fun than a Rubik Cube, because it involves God, me, and others in working out the solution. It never comes out twice the same way because, you see, each one of us is unique, with our own life solution. But it won't work unless God—and others—are a part of it.

The Interior Life

Do you remember the phrase "the interior life"? It was a common one in spiritual books a few decades ago.

St. Paul paints a vivid picture of a kind of battle going on inside each of us, a sort of tugging back and forth between good and evil. He describes himself as pulled one way by his "lower nature" and then somehow brought back to balance by some good push or shove. More often, people do not take time out to reflect on what is going on inside of them. They are too preoccupied, too busy. St. Ambrose compared these to people who go far away from themselves, like the prodigal son, but in a spiritual, more than a physical, sense. It sometimes happens that suddenly a tragedy, a shock, will bring them back to reality and force them to reflect on their lives.

Although St. Paul was aware of the tug-of-war within himself, he was never discouraged or depressed. He knew that the grace of God swayed the balance toward good. He knew that redemption means that the love of Christ would pull him through.

Some spiritual writers compared the interior life to a kind of block of wood or marble not yet sculpted. Out of it we—but not alone—can create a masterpiece. Out of chaos God created order, and it was good. We know from psychology that the inner chaos is confusing and complex—perhaps even frightening at times—but it is what Jesus came to redeem, not some abstract humanity way out there in space. Jesus loves that chaos which is I!

Perhaps a better image than marble or wood would be clay—but an ever-flexible, pliant, formable mass, capable of infinite shapes and creative wonders. On that chaos God breathes his Spirit at baptism to transform it into the image of his Son.

The interior life is the world within, where the Spirit dwells and moves and shapes and tugs—and probably chuckles a bit in the process at some of the crazy, distorted shapes our character assumes. Some people do not know of that world within, because they take no time to reflect or to be quiet and just be.

Perhaps the most important sentiment we must have is awe: wonder at God's ways within us. He formed us out of the clay of the earth, each one different. His grace continues to transform all of us into the finest sculptured garden this Eden-world has ever known.

God on Our Side

All of us, at one time or another, have heard people say that they cannot believe in God because, if God existed and were all powerful and all good, how could he then permit so much suffering in the world? He would surely stop it. The answer usually given by theologians is that God created the human person with free will and thus he has to respect the nature of the human person. He could not create us free and then take over. He expects us to use our talents and free will to create an equitable and just society.

But there is more to it than that kind of philosophical answer. Although it is correct, it does not tell the whole story. Revelation tells us that God is also a God of love and very concerned about us and what happens on this earth. He did not abandon us to our own devices. He decided to show his weight on our side—out of love for us. For this reason he did not abandon his people or this world and its history, but continued to be part of it—leaving us, however, always free to accept or reject his loving, helping hand. That loving intervention in history reached its culmination in the birth of Jesus, in his sacrificial death, in his victorious resurrection, in the sending of his Spirit to be with us till the end of time. That loving intervention resulted in more than a helping hand; it consists in giving us a share in divine life. For those who believe, it is also a sharing in his own creative life. Yet he leaves us free.

But, again, he tipped the scale in our favor. Without touching that freedom, he gave us the command to pray for our needs, to knock persistently and the door would be opened. It is prayer which tips the balance in our favor. He hears our prayers. In fact, he teaches us how to pray. But we should not see God as sitting there waiting for us to pray so that he can feel okay about undoing our freedom. No. That freedom remains. We exercise it when we pray. We exercise it also in our doing. He answers those prayers in subtle ways and according to our needs. He also answers our prayers by leading us slowly to do the right thing. He never ceases to be a loving God. He never becomes machine-like or mechanical in answering our prayers. He always remains personal. His answer is personal just as his sending of Jesus, his Son, was a *personal* intervention in our history.

I am not trying to explain away the mystery of prayer and how it acts upon God's free will; but he told us of the importance of prayer in forming our personal relationship with him, and so that should be enough for us. We are not abandoned in our search for him and his justice. He is present in all our struggles, in all our joys. Since he wants to share them with us, he asks us to pray.

What a powerful thought! We have God as a partner! Or are we his? Be with us, Lord.

Being Angry at God

Whenever the psalmist cries out to God in times of distress, he does so, as a rule, with respect and filial piety. On the other hand, there are times—take for example Psalm 77—when the bitterness of the psalmist for being abandoned by God shows forth. God is far away, disinterested in the plight of his faithful one: why doesn't he wake up and act?

Can you imagine being angry at God? Of course, the psalmist eventually comes around to remembering all the good things God did in the past for his people; he recalls so many instances of his love, and finally finds new hope in the present. Still, for a moment or for even a much longer time, real anger is present.

I have met a lot of people who were angry at God but they felt inhibited to talk about it. Such feelings can follow what seemed to be a senseless or premature death of a son, a daughter, a friend, or a spouse. Why did God pick on me? Why does he have to be so cruel and inconsistent? Or perhaps we say: "I prayed and prayed and I lit candles and I went to Mass and I gave money in the poor box, and still he didn't hear me." Occasionally people with handicaps, those who must face life with so many disadvantages, express such anger. Why must they go through life scarred and the wicked seem to get all the breaks?

Is it wrong to get angry at God?

Jesus got angry with injustice whenever he saw it around him, so I feel that such emotions in us are also instinctive "Christian" reactions to what we feel are injustices against us. I guess I would have to say that the feelings are natural and that it would be healthy for us to recognize them as such.

Staying in the state of bitterness and anger is not good for anyone, so we, too, must be like the psalmist and try to turn that anger into a broader vision in prayer. We, too, must reflect on all those aspects of Scripture which show us a loving, caring God who has more than just a superficial interest in our well-being. Even though we know that God loves us, it is still possible to get angry at those we love, and, thus, at God. In fact, sometimes I wonder if he is not even flattered and glad we are doing so.

Have you ever seen a little child, tired and peevish, lash out at a parent, only to be swept up and caressed? Perhaps God is even saying to us: "Take it out on me—not on all those people around you. You won't hurt me. And when you get it out of your system, I will take you up in my arms. There you can have a good cry and be at peace."

Inwardness

One of the greatest surprises which came to me as a novice was to learn that God truly dwells within us. Perhaps I had known this theoretically much earlier in life, but the full impact of the doctrine only came with a certain maturity.

It was explained to us by the novice master that with the gift of created grace there came the indwelling of the uncreated God. I recall how he read to us a passage from St. Basil the Great to explain that overwhelming doctrine. Basil had said it was like a seal pressed into flowing water. The water remained water, but took on the form of the seal. So our souls remained truly themselves, but, so intimately touched by God, they were formed to his image.

In addition to this important doctrine one should also reflect on the very special union which is created between Jesus and the human person who at Mass receives the body and blood of Christ. There is no doubt that, although the person might be fully united to God, a very special relationship of presence with Jesus is effected. It is both real and sacramental. It is also true that Communion effects a new and real relationship at Mass among all those participating, since they all share in that one unique presence of Jesus. This is why the thanksgiving after Communion can never be only personal but must include the post-Communion prayer which brings out the communal and interpersonal union with Jesus.

All of us can say that in our lives we have had moments in which the presence of God or of Jesus has been truly experienced and felt. At other times it is only in the depth of faith that we are aware of that real presence within us and must rest in the assurance that, although unexperienced, God is truly present.

Cultivating such inwardness can be a help to our prayer in four different ways.

Inwardness makes spontaneous prayer easier. When we are aware that God is so intimately present to us, we can more easily and more freely talk to him in our own words as we would friend to friend or lover to lover.

Inwardness also facilitates moments of quiet meditation and contemplation. Unlike many Oriental methods which end in or seek a kind of emptiness or nothingness, the Christian becomes in quietude always more aware of the living presence of God within. Few words, if any, may be spoken, but the presence remains a reality in which one rests.

Inwardness also makes it easier to seek forgiveness; in fact, it makes such a request for forgiveness imperative. But one does not in such inwardness rest in a state of abjection and guilt because of sin. The positive real presence helps beget courage and hope.

A cultivation of a sense of that inward presence of God is also a great help for participation in liturgy. At times during the liturgy it is impossible to focus on everything that happens and to follow in detail everything that is said. Sometimes the liturgy is too dense for immediate absorption. In these cases inwardness remains a binding force through all diversity.

Inwardness, or that sense and belief that God is within me, can be cultivated, if only I seek to do so.

Transformation

Frequently people ask me about books which have affected my life. One always comes to mind: *Christ Our*

Brother by Karl Adam. Some priest gave it to me to read when I was a sophomore in college and it left a powerful impression on me. It opened new ways of seeing Christ and stimulated new dimensions of prayer.

Somehow, up to that point, the humanity of Jesus had not taken hold of me. I suppose I still thought of Jesus in too spiritualistic a fashion. I probably, secretly and involuntarily, was a bit of an Apollinarist (one of those fourth century heretics who denied Jesus had a human soul). Affirming his total humanity did not deny or diminish his divinity, I had to learn. It was only after reading Adam's book that I saw what I was missing. Jesus was completely and totally human—like me. It doesn't say in the Gospel that he had a runny nose when he was a child and headaches when he was a teenager and backaches when he carpentered too long as an adult—but why not?

Later I read St. Thomas Aquinas and found out how important that humanity of Jesus was—body and soul. So many passages of Scripture, especially the accounts of the passion and death, make no sense without focusing on the fullness of Jesus' humanity. Jesus was not a kind of humanoid robot being manipulated by some divine hidden strings. He was totally like us. The Fathers of the Church and the theologians exempted him from sin and sinful passions. That was okay by me, provided the fullness of humanity was there. The divine, they pointed out, did not supplant some part of his human nature.

But St. Thomas Aquinas went even further and talked about Jesus *in his humanity* as being now for all of us for all eternity the permanent access of our finite being and humanity to the living God of infinite, eternal life. That, to me, could be the object of endless thought!

When the Gospel says that Jesus was raised from the dead, it means the whole man, body and soul. He wanted the apostle Thomas to touch that body and see the same marks on his hands and in his side. Yes, the same body— even if somehow transformed.

Because of our own incorporation into Christ at baptism, the feast of the resurrection is also a celebration of our own humanity, of our own flesh. We, too, are made up of body and soul. Resurrection means not just resurrection of the soul but of our wholeness. We do not just save our soul, but are totally healed, totally saved. From this doctrine can be deduced the beauty and respect of the human body as well as the soul. The mission of the Church and of salvation is to the entire person. Original sin might have weakened our nature, but the Church has always taught us about its basic goodness, that it remains fundamentally unimpaired. I can say to myself: "This body, and none other, will be resurrected; God must indeed see it as good."

The Church today has been very conscious of the beauty of the human person and the value and worth of the whole person—body and soul. Words which formerly seemed negative—like sexuality—now carry a positive ring. So many consequences follow from this perception, too many for one meditation. However, in the Easter season, when we contemplate the risen Lord in the fullness of his humanity transformed, we can look forward in hope to the total transformation of our own humanity—when, like his, it will become radiant with the presence of the living God.

Take a moment now to touch your body and say to yourself: this body is indeed good and in the sight of God highly redeemable.

Piety

Piety is not one of our favorite words these days. To call someone pious or devout is no longer a compliment. What has happened to bring about this change? Why has piety acquired a pejorative meaning?

Piety seems often to suggest an attitude of immaturity, of being out of touch with reality, of being naive. Piety has also come to be associated with sham, showy, exterior signs without genuine holiness, that often hide insincerity, egoism, an individualism which does not see the needs of others.

Yet something seems to be missing in our present religious attitudes where there is no piety. According to anthropologists, piety is deep-seated in the human person and expresses that attitude of wonder and awe before God and the divine. It is the exterior comportment that follows deep belief. True piety is mature and spontaneous.

Ironically enough, we have rediscovered the role of the body and its importance for worship. The wholeness of the human person is a constant theme in our present spirituality. But we haven't yet discovered the need for piety. Perhaps one of our inhibitions comes from the fear of being ridiculed by our peers. The enemy of true piety is mockery and ridicule. The American Church, in particular, has an overdose at this moment of spiritual snobbery which engages in sophisticated—and often offensive—ridicule in order to seem cute. There are several Catholic periodicals which specialize in such ridicule, and not to laugh means not to be "with it." These periodicals never seem to know the fine line between good humor and just bad taste. (Bishops seem most often to receive the brunt of such ridicule. Or am I becoming too sensitive?)

Christ, too, was aware of false piety and external show in religion and excoriated those Pharisees who sought applause for their external acts. Our piety, he warns us, has to be tested for its genuineness. That is one of the purposes of Lent. The liturgy in these weeks helps us see ourselves as we are, but also as we could be without God's sustaining, caring, loving support. From these attitudes will rise a true piety—which is the expression of our dependence on God, but also of the dignity to which he has called us.

If we have succumbed to the temptation of ridiculing others for their piety, perhaps we should examine if that ridicule might not be an escape for us. The mockery might be hiding our own state of discomfort in that we are not being consequential in our beliefs. Lent is a moment of grace for all of us, a moment to get in touch again with God and the real believing "us." We might even become pious and devout again—even if no one knows.

Stability

In 1980 we Benedictines celebrated the 1,500th anniversary of the birth of St. Benedict. When an institution has survived as many ups and downs in history as our order has, one naturally asks: To what can this longevity be attributed?

There are many possible answers in this case, but I would like to point out just one. St. Benedict introduced into monasticism a concept of stability which had not been there before. The monks still take that additional vow of stability.

I have singled out this element, not only because of its importance for the history of monasticism, but also because, through it, the monks, too, contributed to civilization. It still has a message for all of us.

At the time Benedict wrote his Rule, Western civilization was in shambles. The tribes from the north had descended over the Roman Empire, and the great upheaval we know as the barbarian invasion had left the known world in a state of chaos. Such an upheaval had affected people's lives in many ways, not just materially, but also psychologically and spiritually. People couldn't "settle down."

There are so many aspects of the times of Benedict which remind us of our own day. People then tended to be nomadic; they were constantly on the go. We are much like them. Although we often have a spot to come home to, still our culture is a restless one, full of constant new stimuli and experiences. Even monks at the time of Benedict were more like hippies on the move; Benedict called them gyrovagues. Restless spirits, they wandered from place to place. Benedict hints that they thus never grew up, never faced the challenge of living through and working through crises and problems, but always evaded them. For this reason he demanded that his monks settle down, join a stable community under a stable authority. They thus became wedded to the locality and to the land. He makes provisions for monks on journeys (he knew there would be reasons for them at times to be out of the cloister), but even those rules were aimed at keeping the monk spiritually and psychologically at rest.

Historians often have remarked that monasticism has flourished best when there were moments of cultural upheaval. At those moments stability becomes more important than usual and helps the monastery not just to survive, but to contribute to the forming of a new culture.

What has stability to say to all of us today? Very much, I believe. We all must settle down, sink roots, and stop this endless foolish motion. It has affected us psychologically and spiritually. One cannot pray, one cannot reflect, one cannot grow, if one is in perpetual motion. Stability is an attitude of mind; it is not just physical. As stable people we can become truly concerned about our family, our neighborhood, our city. We begin to shape our lives through stable relationships; we begin to contribute to the well-being of those around us; we cease looking for distractions. Calming ourselves down and sinking roots is truly good for the soul. Let us not be spiritual gyrovagues.

Sensitivity and Sanctity

Some people by nature tend to be extremely sensitive. It is not just that they are easily hurt but they also sense the hurts of society and of others very profoundly. Sensitive people seem to be able to pick out in a group, before others do, those who are suffering, those who have been offended, those who are timid, those who are ill-at-ease. It seems to be second nature to them. Sensitive people seem to wear their emotions on their sleeves. It is not that they are sentimental or cry easily—often they are the more restrained and don't give in to emotional outbursts. It is just that their emotional nature responds rapidly and fully to even the slightest joy and suffering which is genuine and unaffected.

Artists must be sensitive people if they are to be effective in their art. They not only must experience human emotion deeply but they must be able to communicate it to others through their artistic medium. Art, we know, can never be just logic and mathematics.

Sanctity, too, requires that same kind of sensitivity. Jesus became human like us. He must have been the most sensitive of persons. Witness how often he was moved to pity by the sorrow and pain of others. We see him bringing back to life the son of the widow of Naim because he was moved by pity. We see him raising Lazarus from the dead, having been moved to tears at the news of his death. We find him again moved with pity for the starving crowds and feeding them. That same sensitivity found him going out to the sick, the crippled, the destitute—even to the point of death on the cross. Jesus must have been a very sensitive person indeed.

How many saints could be brought forward as examples of that same kind of sensitivity! All the renowned contemplatives in the history of Christianity strike us as very sensitive persons, full of overflowing love. There is Augustine—what an example of a delicate artist able to express deep emotion and tenderness! Thomas Aquinas, Francis of Assisi, Bernard of Clairvaux, and John of the Cross come immediately to mind from that same mystical tradition. Of particular importance are the women: Teresa of Avila, Gertrude, Thérèse of the Child Jesus (The Little Flower), Catherine of Siena, and so on. Other saints showed their extreme sensitivity by creating apostolates and means to help the destitute. There is a long line of such compassionate saints: Damian (the leper), Vincent de Paul, Camillus de Lellis, the foundresses of so many congregations of sisters, even to our own Mother Teresa of Calcutta. All of you could easily compose your own list.

Perhaps sensitive people wish they could be a bit more callous, a bit harder, a bit more firm. On the contrary, they should thank God for that sensitivity, for it is a gift, a grace, a means of special sanctity. The world today is crying out for such a kind of sensitivity, for people who understand, for people who feel deeply the anguish which others suffer and which words do not adequately express. We live in a world callous by structure and size and anonymity. We do not need more of that. Martyrs are always needed, but perhaps suffering, sensitive saints are more helpful today.

Would I be out of line in challenging especially the women of the Church today to such a kind of sanctity? To them, in particular, I would say: Be sensitive, accept the suffering that goes with such a nature, accept it as a gift and a grace, so you can be more Christ-like and bear him to others in need, as Mary did.

Spiritual Burnout

In reading one of Dietrich Bonhoeffer's letters when he was in prison during the Nazi period (March 19, 1944), I was struck by his honesty in admitting that he was finding it difficult to read the Bible. He admitted to this periodic problem, decided that it would be wrong to get upset about it, "for better to trust that, after wobbling a bit, the compass will come to rest in the right direction." Bonhoeffer was noticing an old ailment which spiritual writers have talked about since the beginning of Christianity. The early monks of the desert called it *akedia,* listless, lazy distractedness, that noonday devil that could get many a monk into trouble. If it lasted for a period of time, later authors used more descriptively psychological terms: dryness, dark night of the soul, emptiness. It is a phenomenon which strikes all those seriously engaged in spiritual pursuits and is especially irksome to middle-aged priests and religious. The spring of the year is a bad time, with so many Masses and ceremonies. Sometimes it happens after major feasts, such as Christmas and Easter: one just can't face one more liturgy or prayer-sharing.

At times it happens in the quiet of one's room: God is just far away—no feeling of his presence, no tricks to conjure up that good inner feeling of his abiding love. For some such a state can last a long time, even though faith is strong and the yearning for his presence is genuine and deep. If it lasts too long, it can lead to a "spiritual burnout." Priests, in particular, have to be aware of this danger, because they are constantly under the stress and tension which accompany the ministry of word and sacrament, and counseling and praying. Perhaps our laity have not been sympathetic enough in recognizing this syndrome in their priests—and in themselves.

But to all I say, "Cheer up. It can only happen to the good." You see, it is a malady which cannot strike those who are not conscientious. It is like a runner's leg cramp; it is not an armchair disease. And like the runner's leg cramp, it is a warning to slow down, stop overexerting, and let time take out the kinks. Usually the origins of incipient spiritual burnout are over physical, psychological, and spiritual strain and tiredness. It is too much of a good thing. We can't always be breaking spiritual Olympic records.

It is also a way of getting a fresh start. It forces us off our feet and back to human reality again. We see our own limitations and accept them. From that realization comes new growth and a fresh start. The formula for a cure should be to begin to rely a bit more on God's providence and a bit less on self. Take a bit of distance from the spirituality—a quiet retreat, or just a good novel. Examine one's spiritual diet and bring it back into line again; perhaps a bit more solitude and silence is needed, fewer words, slower reading, less talking.

Then be open to new events and new people that suddenly break upon us. It only takes a spark to ignite a new zeal and ardor in us if we are waiting in such a quiet, listening pose. The burnout turns then to a warm charcoal glow.

Boredom

I will never forget old Fr. Bernardine. He already had retired when I was a young monk, if monks really retire; perhaps I should say that he no longer had a regular assignment. For a short time he had been pastor of a small one-man parish. (That job didn't last long, because he couldn't balance a checkbook and he complained to the abbot that the housekeeper knew no Greek!) But I thought he knew everything, because he could converse about literature (in any language), music, art, history—you name it.

One day he told me that he never knew what it meant to be bored. He had so many things he wanted to do in life that time was not sufficient. But he always had time for every monk who dropped in to his cell to discuss just about anything. (For a while he was engaged in a vigorous contest with Fr. Eric to see who could find the raciest Latin passages in the Fathers!)

I thought of Fr. Bernardine again recently when I heard several teenagers say how bored they were. They went to the movies and an hour later they were bored. They watched television and they were bored. What else is there to do but jump in the car and seek excitement? It seems that we try in our society to raise "creative" children—so our schools say. But do we create truly curious children? Somewhere along the line we stifle that natural intellectual curiosity which is so necessary for a full life.

I have no remedy for teenage boredom. We are so accustomed now to live on emotional "highs" that between peaks we are bored. We all know what happens then. The "highs" must always become higher (since they lose their punch and the periods between peaks are shortened), lest boredom sets in. These syndromes have a disastrous effect on our spiritual life, too. Spiritually one cannot live on a constant high. We become like those disbelievers whom Jesus chides because they are always seeking miracles and signs and wonders. Religion can so easily be reduced to only emotional stimuli.

The remedy can come from the Gospel message—although perhaps it would be difficult to convince teenagers and others of this. First of all, the Gospel presents to us the mystery of each individual person. Those who learn to appreciate this mystery never get bored; new aspects of the people we know and love are like a never-ending kaleidoscope. For the Gospel, the work to be done of transforming this world into a just society, the kind which Jesus tells us he came to esablish, never ends, and every attempt to get involved opens new wonders and mysteries.

For the Christian, God's creation is full of newness at every turn. Understanding that creation and learning how to use it creatively is an ongoing task. There is so much to know, so much to do, so much to care about! What is missing in the lives of so many is not the search for emotional fulfillment but the neglect of the intellect, the brain, the understanding. If that part of us has not been developed, life will indeed be boredom. If we live only on emotion, it becomes the size of the dose which counts and we lose all sense of nuance and quality and delicateness.

As Fr. Bernardine would say: "If you love God's creatures and his creation and are concerned about more than self-gratification, life will be full of wonders and surprises, like a new Mozart symphony every day."

Forgiveness

It was Peter who asked Jesus how many times we should forgive those who offend us (Mt 18:21). Could he have foreseen that Jesus would have to forgive him more than once for his cowardice? Jesus put no limit on the number of times. But he did tell his disciples the parable of the unjust servant, the one who was forgiven by his master but did not forgive his fellow servant. By this parable Jesus reminds us how much we were forgiven. We should never forget our own need to be forgiven.

First of all, God has forgiven us many times over. He is a patient, loving God, always ready to pardon, always ready to receive us prodigals back. The history of God's people shows our God to be a faithful, loving, merciful Lord. We have often been forgiven by others, too. If we would only think back a bit over our past, especially when we were young, and reflect on our selfishness and self-centeredness, we should recall how often we were thoughtless, weak, and even malicious. Often we were in need of forgiveness. It is so easy to forget the offenses of our youth. Often the wildest kids grow up to be the most unbending and unforgiving of parents. Then, too, we have to resist the temptation of wanting to "get even." Our society does not have a tradition of enduring family vengeances, but, deep down in each one of us, there is a tendency to want to see others punished.

It is also most difficult to be the first to forgive: it seems "unmanly." After a quarrel it is always a problem who gives in first. We tend to go on forever explaining, justifying our side of the question, more to convince ourselves than anyone else. It is not easy to ask for forgiveness. Such an act requires humility and a higher perspective. But there are moments when we must muster the courage and admit the need to seek reconciliation.

What is truly a sign of maturity and growth is our ability to see other people's goodness and weakness and to attribute to them good motives, so that we are not constantly going through those adolescent moods of being offended. Having confidence that others truly love us, we will not be easily offended.

The most important message from Jesus' love for us which we should understand and apply in our own lives is that he loved us in our weakness. He did not wait till we deserved his love—he would have waited forever—but came to us because we are weak and in need of his presence. To accept people as they are, who they are, and to love them in their imperfections—that is to be Christ-like, to imitate Christ's love for us. For that love we can be thankful and we can take seriously his example: forgive us our trespasses as we forgive those who trespass against us!

Witnessing

A new word has come into our Catholic vocabulary: we must be *witnesses* to our faith in Jesus.

Actually it is an old word, but one which was somewhat avoided because it seemed to be the domain of the Reformed Churches. We probably were afraid to use it, lest we sounded "Protestant." On the other hand, it is such an important word in the New Testament and in the spirituality of the early Church that we cannot lose this precious heritage: instead, we must reclaim it as our own. (The Greek word for witness is martyr!)

Jesus is the faithful witness to the truth and bears witness of what he has seen and heard from his Father (Jn 3:11). His works, accomplished at the command of the Father, witness to his mission (Jn 5:36; 10:25).

The disciples of Jesus became witnesses because they were to carry the Gospel message, the good news, into the whole world (Mt 24:14). They were to attest before all people to the events between the baptism of Jesus until his ascension. As witnesses, they also were to expect to suffer for his sake, for his name's sake. Stephen was the first to seal his witness by shedding his blood for the faith (Acts 22:20).

As followers of Christ, we, too, must be witnesses. To do so adequately, three things are necessary.

First of all, we must know about Jesus. The one to take the place of Judas had to have been a witness of what Jesus did and said from his baptism till the ascension. To grow in the knowledge of Jesus means to reflect on his word—the Bible—to be a person of prayer, to spend time with him; thus, our knowledge will be more than theoretical information. It also means being attentive to his presence in others and in events. All of these help us know Jesus so that we can be his living witnesses.

Second, we witness through the truthfulness of our lives. By that I mean that we must develop a real and authentic relationship between our values, our ideals, and how we act. Facades are easily forced to crumble. We witness by the sincerity of our being. Christ must shine through us.

Third, it is clear from the Gospel that witnessing involves, too, the willingness to make sacrifices, to pay the "price" of being Jesus' disciple. How often Jesus warns us that the world will not treat the servant better than the master. We must be willing to suffer for our convictions. That is an integral part of witnessing.

In the early Church martyrdom was seen as the highest form of witnessing, because it was the most complete way of imitating Jesus who gave up his life as a witness of his Father's love for us. We are not called to such extreme form of witnessing, but must do so daily in little things. We must grow in the knowledge of who Jesus is, become more like him in our attitudes toward his Father, our brothers and sisters, and this world, and be willing to suffer so that his Kingdom can come about. Through baptism and confirmation we are called to be that kind of witness.

Faith and Community

During the synod of bishops in 1974 on the theme of evangelization, a term much discussed was *communidades eclesiales de base*—basic Christian communities or grass-roots communities. Bishops from Africa, Asia, and especially South America cited the many benefits which have accrued to their dioceses, almost spontaneously, through this movement to break parishes down into smaller units for prayer and meditation on the Gospel.

When Pope Paul VI gathered together all the reflections of the bishops of that synod in his powerful apostolic exhortation on Evangelization in the Modern World, *Evangelii Nuntiandi* (December 8, 1975), he devoted a section to this new pastoral means—smaller basic communities. The best summary of those paragraphs was given by Pope John Paul II in an address he delivered in Mexico City to the National Catholic Organizations of Mexico (January 29, 1979). He said:

> One of the phenomena of recent years which has manifested with ever-increasing vigor the dynamism of the laity in Latin America and elsewhere has been that of the so-called grass-roots communities *(communautes de base),* which have arisen coincidentally with the crisis of the movement toward groupings among Catholics.
>
> The grass-roots communities can be a valid instrument of formation and of religious life within a new environment of Christian impulse, and they can be useful, among other things, for a widespread penetration of the Gospel in society.
>
> But that this may be possible it is necessary that they bear well in mind the criteria so clearly expressed by the

apostolic exhortation *Evangelii Nuntiandi* (58), so that they may be nourished by the word of God in prayer, and remain united, not separated, and still less in opposition to the Church, to the pastors, and to other ecclesial groups or associations.

In praising this phenomenon of the breaking into smaller communities, Pope Paul points out how they can be a real hope for the Church, local and universal, and cause it to grow. He was, of course, aware of the dangers if such communities claim to have a monopoly on the Spirit, degenerate into political or ideological factions, become sectarian. If, on the other hand, they are nourished by God's word and remain firmly attached to the local Church and its pastors, to the universal Church and its magisterium, then these basic church-communities, he states, will fulfill their vocation: "As hearers of the Gospel which is proclaimed to them and privileged beneficiaries of evangelization, they will soon become proclaimers of the Gospel themselves" (58).

The early Church grew up around "domestic" churches, "family-groupings," and so this phenomenon is not a new one. Reflecting on the Gospel together, praying together, sharing insights on how that Gospel message challenges the modern world—all of these are ways of growing in holiness.

The Spirit is calling us to such sharing; may we grow because of it. Then we will be ready for the next stage. Pope Paul described it as the way in which a Christian community, having assimilated the Gospel message, seeks, without betraying in the least the essential truth of the Gospel, to proclaim and communicate that message to others. Lord, make us into worthy recipients of your message of love!

Lord, make us worthy transmitters of that message to all people!

Interlude

Mary, the Faithful One

Was Mary present on Pentecost? Most artists and iconographers show her among the group as tongues of fire came to rest on each one present. The evidence for her presence is found in the first chapter of the Acts of the Apostles. The apostles had returned to Jerusalem from the Mount of Olives, where the ascension had taken place, and had gathered in the upper room. Their names are then listed. The text which follows says others were present: "Together they devoted themselves to constant prayer. There were some women in their company, and Mary the mother of Jesus, and his brothers" (Acts 1:14).

Next follows the story of the election of Matthias to take the place of Judas. Chapter 2 begins with the account of Pentecost: "When the day of Pentecost came it found them gathered in one place" (Acts 2:1). It can be presupposed that Mary is still among them. This passage, however, is the last account we have in the New Testament of her presence. Luke does not mention that Mary was at the foot of the cross (we know this from John), and so there is special interest in his recounting that she was alive and a part of the first faith-community after the resurrection and ascension as they waited and prayed for the coming of the Holy Spirit.

It was only fitting that she should be present for the beginning of the Church on Pentecost, because Luke describes her earlier in the infancy section of his Gospel as the first believer, the first disciple. Chapter 1 of his Gospel tells the story of the angel Gabriel appearing to her and announcing that she would bear a son and give him the name of Jesus. To allay her doubts and fears, the angel insisted: "The Holy Spirit will come upon you and the power of the Most High will overshadow you" (Lk 1:35). Mary answers as the truly obedient disciple: "I am the servant of the Lord. Let it be done to me as you say" (Lk 1:38). She heard God's word and was obedient to it. The Magnificat, the hymn of praise which she then utters, shows her as the one to represent all of God's poor (the anawim): "He has looked upon his servant in her lowliness; all ages to come shall call me blessed" (Lk 1:48).

In this scene Mary acts as figure and type of the believing Christian community. She sees herself among the lowly and poor but as especially loved and chosen by God; she believes when she hears his word and is obedient to it. Later, in chapter 8 Luke tells us that Jesus was surrounded by a crowd, and his mother and brothers came to be with him but could not reach him. Jesus says to those telling him that they are outside: "My mother and my brothers are those who hear the word of God and act upon it" (Lk 8:21).

In a similar vein, Luke tells us that once, when Jesus was preaching, a woman from the crowd called out, "Blest is the womb that bore you and the breast that nursed you!" "Rather," he replied, "blest are they who hear the word of God and keep it" (Lk 11:27–28).

All these pictures Luke draws of Mary show her as a true disciple, one obedient to God's Word. So that there could be no misunderstanding, however, he explicitly numbers her among those forming the first community of believers—the Church. By so doing he lets us know that Mary persevered in that belief, accepting the mystery of the words spoken to her by Simeon of a sword piercing her heart (Lk

2:34–35) and the words Jesus spoke to her after being found in the temple (Lk 2:49). Mary is shown by Luke not only as the first disciple but also as the faithful one—the one whose life spans all the years and events from the birth of Christ to the birth of the Church. The same dramatic intervention of the Spirit is evident in both "births." No wonder the angel called her "full of grace."

Mary: A Prayer

Dear Mary, how did you feel inside when the angel Gabriel announced that you were about to be the mother of the Savior (Lk 1:26–38)? You showed you were flabbergasted that God loved a nobody like you so much. You were dumbfounded that he asked for your okay, your *fiat.*

Mary, teach me to be open to God's ways in my life and to say my "yes" to him.

† † †

Dear Mary, how did you react when Elizabeth, your cousin, declared you the most blessed among women (Lk 1:39–56)? You were so full of joy and happiness for her and for all the marvelous things God was doing that you had to share them. You were the first evangelist, the first to spread the good news.

Mary, teach me how to share joy with others and to praise God for his goodness to me.

† † †

Dear Mary, when Simeon said that a sword would pierce your heart, how did you react to the prediction that you had to be the mother of a suffering Savior (Lk 2:22–39)? You accepted the fact that to be the light of the nations Jesus would have to be rejected by many, too. You accepted that deep suffering also would come to you because you were his mother.

Mary, teach me to accept purifying suffering and not to forget the light of resurrection.

† † †

Dear Mary, how frightened you must have been when Jesus had strayed from the crowd and was lost in the temple (Lk 2:41–52)! Jesus made it clear that his duty came first. He put the work of his Father before all else. You responded to this example by keeping all of these events in your heart, shrouded as they were in the mystery of God's will.

Mary, teach me to put God's point of view first in my life and to be ready to sacrifice for his Kingdom, even when I don't understand.

† † †

Dear Mary, were you embarrassed that perhaps you had spoken out of turn at Cana when you mentioned to Jesus that the wine had run out (Jn 2:1–5)? Jesus' answer to you seemed strange: "Woman, how does that concern of yours involve me? My hour has not yet come." But you must have known that even before his final hour of glory he would manifest—if only in a small way—his power to transform. You had confidence.

Mary, teach me to be unselfish in asking for others and for their needs and to have confidence in the power of your Son to change me and this world.

† † †

Dear Mary, were you hurt or offended when Jesus, having been asked who were his mother and brothers, answered that all who believe and do the will of God were his mother and brothers (Mk 3:31–35)? It must have been hard for you, Mary, to accept the detachment Jesus had to show toward you and his relatives. Did you then fully understand that his mission and role was not a "family affair"? He had to make that clear, even if it seemed cruel.

Mary, teach me to be detached from all that would impede my vision of what God wants of me.

✝ ✝ ✝

Dear Mary, as you stood under the cross and heard Jesus give you to John as mother, did you wince at losing your only Son and at having no relatives to take you in (Jn 19:25–27)? You may have been aware then that his hour had come and that this gesture, simple in itself, was also a sign that he was giving you a new place as mother of the Church, as mother of us all.

Mary, teach me to be persevering, to stay beside the cross and to trust in God's providential ways in my own life, because Jesus is my brother and you are my mother.

Amen.

Liturgy and Spirituality

A Prayer To Begin: Dying and Rising

Lord Jesus, you had to die. In becoming a human being like us you did not exempt yourself from that event that is most human—that is, dying.

Yet, in the Gospel narrative by St. John, you are always Lord of death. You lay down your life in response to your Father's will. Death, according to John, is that sinful state which separates from God, which drags us down, which leaves us a prey to the flesh, to the powers of evil. By meeting this kind of sinful death head-on you robbed death of its power, Lord. By emptying yourself for others you made death a way of life. But emptying yourself was done through love. It is love which conquers death. Death is sin and hatred and selfishness. Life is goodness and kindness. This you taught us, Jesus, by example.

You told us, too, dear Lord, if we would come after you, that we must deny ourselves and take up our cross and follow you. How unromantic this is, Jesus! But if your cross is to die to hate and to learn to love as you did, then I see how your yoke could be sweet!

Just as we move daily toward physical death, so, dear Lord, should we be dying to sin. In that way our physical death will be, as in your case, the result of and the sign of an interior dying to self. You taught us, however, Lord, that dying with you means rising with you. Baptism is a cycle; it is entering into your cycle of dying to sin and rising to new life. Our life is not a journey on a continuous path toward inevitable death, but a daily dying and rising. The seed of our dying, Jesus, is creative of new life. When sin and selfishness die, there is room for goodness and joy. When hate dies, there is room for love.

Again, your disciple John wrote: "That we have passed from death to life we know because we love each other. One who does not love is among the living dead" (1 Jn 3:14). The way we came to understand love was that you laid down your life, Jesus, for us; we, too, must lay down our lives for our brothers and sisters.

A Benedictine friend of mine from Arkansas told me the following story, Jesus. You will like it. It took place in the mid-1960's, a time of racial bitterness and violence. A young college graduate was spending his first year out of school working for voter registration among the blacks of eastern Arkansas. It was dangerous work. The monks asked him one day if he had suffered violence because of his efforts. He quietly told of the times he had been beaten with chains, kicked, and spit upon. "Why didn't you fight back?" the monks asked him. "At first I did," he responded. "But then I realized that hate must die. If I respond to hate in kind, it bounces off me back into the world. It continues to arch out and harm people. Somewhere this hate has to come to rest. I know now that I must let it die in my body."

Jesus, let hate die in all our bodies, so that slowly this world can be transformed. Love is born of hate that dies.

Suffering and sadness, morbidity and pessimism are not the story of Good Friday, Lord. Nor is bubbly, flighty giddiness the story of Easter Sunday. Our vibrant joy of Easter will come, Lord, when we have died to violence, hatred, dishonesty, greed, and passion. Teach us the meaning of Good Friday, Jesus, so that we can rise with you each day in Easter joy. Teach us each time we join with others at the Eucharist that it is our Good Friday and Easter Sunday, too. It is our dying and rising. Each sacrament, Lord Jesus, we know is our insertion into your paschal mystery. Keep us aware of you as we bring our daily crosses to be transformed and resurrected.

Amen.

Some General Rules

Liturgical spirituality demands of us a new approach to sign and symbol, one which is not purely ritual performance, but, rather, a gathering point for personal and communal life experience—a point where those life experiences encounter the Christ-event and take on a new meaning and vision.

Signs and symbols in liturgy are not just gathering moments in our religious culture; they also have an objective basis as memorials of Christ's passion, death, and resurrection. For this reason they are not just the spontaneous symbols evolved from one group, but are rooted in historical fact and belong to the whole Church.

Some of these symbols are close to nature—bread, water, wine, fire; others are more difficult to analyze in our present culture—candles, vestments, crosier, miter. Other symbols are not strictly speaking liturgical but lend themselves to devotion and piety—the Sacred Heart. All of these can be helpful for bringing us to a liturgical piety. There seems to be a renewed interest in signs and symbols in our culture (note such movies as E.T. and their popularity), and liturgy should profit from this trend.

One of the aims of the liturgical reform after Vatican II was to make the liturgical signs and rites simple and understandable, unencumbered with gestures which had no meaning. Underneath it all was, in addition, a reaction against baroque triumphalism. Liturgy was not to be just pomp and display, a show, theatricality.

The result after Vatican II was often a kind of empty, jejune, and sterile meeting, where the accent was placed on words, words, words. Or new opportunities for show were invented: long songs after the consecration which ceased to be acclamation and became unending pieces of display that totally interrupted the historical narrative; Communion meditations which were concerts and were just distraction. And so on. Perhaps, however, the greatest weakness was the insensitivity to the other senses. Since people worship with all their being, all senses come into play. Liturgy should not be triumphal, nor pompous, but it must appeal to the eye and nose and ear without being Hollywoodish or maudlin. That is the challenge!

Since Vatican II we have been much aware of music in the liturgy—at least of song. The repertory of "incidental" music, however, has not increased. No one has written, for example, organ interludes based on St. Louis Jesuit melodies. (A Bach would have created a repertory of such needed music by now.) Architecture has fared better. The need to face the people at Mass, to find a place for the presidential chair, and to complete new churches has stimulated a renewal of interest between architecture and liturgy, often with felicitous results. (If I have any complaint here, it is often with the lack of warmth in some new churches. The geometrics are fine, but the atmosphere is not a welcoming one which says: "God is good.")

Perhaps the area which has suffered most in the renewal is that of painting, sculpture, and what often carries the unfortunate title of "decorative arts." On the positive side, there has been a revival of interest in banners and cloth. Recently also we have seen a new interest in vestments with a new realization of their importance. Colors, too, are becoming more subtle. But painting and sculpture have not yet been integrated. All these interests are important and to be encouraged.

Could the return of incense also be a sign that smell should not be forgotten? Incense heightens the importance of a liturgical moment, the proclamation of the Gospel, for example, and adds a new dimension to how the whole person can worship.

Like everyone else, I hope that we are not going to return to pomp for its own sake nor do I want to fall into the TV spectacular mentality; but I do hope the decade of the 1980's will correct some of the sensory deprivation which our liturgy in the 1970's suffered.

There are other aspects of liturgical spirituality which must become a part of our culture and piety. One of these is the way we approach the Bible as a source for our growth in the Spirit. Liturgy is also a spirituality which grows from a sense of community. Our personal piety is challenged by others; we hear God's word together. Finally, liturgy is never separate from life itself and life experiences. Liturgy, thus, by definition is related to the public prayer of the Church; it is not just private devotion. Liturgy has all kinds of support systems. It doesn't just happen on Sunday morning. Liturgy can be and must be nurtured and sustained in the family, the "domestic Church."

The most important aspect of liturgical prayer is that it is always related to the prayer which Jesus offers continually to his Father. Our liturgical prayer is always his prayer. In fact, no one can say "Abba, Father" except in and through him. He is always present to us and presenting our prayer to his Father. Our prayer begins with reflection on his word; hence, the importance of reading the Bible together in the home, reflecting on it, praying it. Our family prayer should also be related to the feasts and liturgical seasons being celebrated by the Church. There are numerous ways of making the Advent, Christmas, Lenten, and Easter seasons meaningful in family prayer. The mysteries of Christ's life and death become central to prayer.

Second, liturgy always involves a community. By its nature liturgy is a group act. It is the prayer of the whole Church realized in this particular limited group. For this reason liturgical prayer is never selfish nor self-contained. It unites us with the other members of the Church. In the family so often prayer is limited to personal devotion. We see the image of the parent assisting the child as the child recites night prayers kneeling at the bedside. This is good. It is important for the child to develop that personal relationship with Jesus and with his Mother. But family prayer must also have the dimension of praying as group. How important it is for children to pray with their parents. This should be the child's first experience of praying as part of a group, a community. In this way the child becomes aware of a praying Church, of which the family is a cell. The child becomes sensitive to the needs of others, of those praying, of those hurting. Here, too, the child sees God as relating to a people, a family, and not just to an individual.

Third, liturgy must be related to life. Our daily life and activity lead up to and away from liturgy. The liturgical act brings together into prayer all our hopes, aspirations, and disappointments; at the same time, it sends us forth as new people to transform this world. Liturgy thus encompasses a continuous, overlapping cycle between life and worship that is always changing and always producing new marvels. For this reason family prayer must take place in an atmosphere of trust and realism. The daily routine of ups and downs, of fears and hopes, of anxieties and joys becomes transformed by prayer. Standard formulas are needed and excellent, but they are not enough. Life must help fertilize prayer; all the heartaches, loves, hurts, and blessings become a part of Jesus' suffering, death, and resurrection. Family prayer then is liberating and freeing, hopeful and trusting. If all of these qualities are nurtured in family prayer, then, surely, the extension of them to the larger community and to the celebration of the Eucharist in particular will be more natural and make our liturgy more understandable and more meaningful.

We have often heard it said: The family that prays together stays together. But I would add: The family that prays together builds Church.

Walking Through the Mass

What should be our disposition as we prepare for the celebration of the Eucharist? What should be in our hearts and in our minds?

Let us begin by remembering that every sacrament is a participation in the great events of Christ's dying and rising again, that which we call the paschal mystery. Every sacrament is a sharing in that mystery, but the Eucharist permits us to do so in the clearest and most striking manner because we believe that the Sacrifice of the Mass is indeed that sacrifice of the cross and all its effects today. At the Eucharist, too, we sense a closeness to Christ and a way of sharing in his life, since he gives us his body to eat and his blood to drink, that is indeed beyond all imagination.

Dying and rising with Christ, however, presupposes on our part a willingness to die to self and sin and to rise to new life. It takes for granted on our part a need and a recognition of the need for the saving graces of redemption. We also are aware that we cannot do it alone; we cannot save ourselves. Only Christ is our Savior, our Redeemer. We must stand before him in our inadequacy, in our need, to be led to his life-giving table.

For this reason we begin each Mass with a penitential rite. Some of this rite had previously been performed in the sacristy as a kind of personal preparation on the part of the celebrant and ministers, but Pope Paul VI intuitively felt that it belonged somehow to the whole congregation. Thus, before the Mass begins, the whole community takes a few seconds to reflect on the need we have for that saving presence of Jesus in our lives. We acknowledge our nothingness, our inadequacies, our inabilities to save ourselves.

It is not a moment for making a laundry list of sins. Thus it is not good liturgy to ask for forgiveness for the number of times we have done this or that wrong. It is not an occasion to dwell on our sins. On the contrary, it is an occasion to dwell on God's mercy, on his love, and on those many manifestations of his love which make us full of hope that those same qualities will be operative in our midst now. Therefore, we say: Lord Jesus, who showed mercy to sinners, who came to bring back the lost sheep, who never ceases to love us, who died for us, and so on.

As happens so often in liturgy, the people's prayers are addressed to Christ while the priest's are offered to God the Father. This is another indication that the *Lord, have mercy* was and is a people's prayer which they should not be deprived of. Thus, the Mass begins each time with a few moments for all of us to remember our need for God in our lives and to recall his love and mercy toward us. This gives us the hope and courage to enter fully into the mystery of his dying and rising again and our dying to sin and rising to new life.

◆

Some documents since Vatican II rather got lost in the shuffle because of the volume of documents to be read or because they seemed too theoretical. In 1981 a new edition of the Lectionary for the Mass appeared. It had few changes from the 1969 edition except for an enlarged preface. That preface is indeed a hidden gem. It points out, first of all, that in every celebration of the liturgy of every sacrament, and especially the Eucharist, the proclamation of the word of God is not only present but significant. Somehow the Holy Spirit works within the believers as they hear that word and respond anew to it.

Every time we hear God's word at Mass, for example, we hear it differently. It may be a text we have heard before, but we hear it in a new moment of our personal life-journey and at a new juncture in the history of the community we are worshiping with. Each hearing of Scripture at worship is a new event for that reason and a new enrichment of our lives. Sometimes we are tired when we hear it, sometimes hurting, sometimes excited or elated. Each time, thus, it can stir our heart and mind in a different way. To me it is like hearing a piece of music one knows well but hearing it in a different atmosphere, by a different performer. The interpretation is always new and revealing; each time is a discovery.

For this reason the word proclaimed in liturgy is called "living" or "active." Somehow God uses that word to effect, under the action of the Spirit, a change, a conversion in us. In this sense the word proclaimed to us awaits a response. We listen. We are affected. We must say our "yes" to that word. Our "yes" cannot just be lip service but must cause us to be doers of the word and not just hearers. The document cited above puts it this way: "The faithful's participation in the liturgy increases to the degree that as they listen to the word of God spoken in the liturgy they strive harder to commit themselves to the word of God made flesh in Christ. They endeavor to conform their way of life to what they celebrate in the liturgy, and then in turn to bring to the celebration of the liturgy all that they do in life" (#6). Each time a group of baptized gather, are called, as Church, and hear the word of God proclaimed, it experiences that it is a new people, a people with a history touched by God's love, a people remade through the death and resurrection of Christ. Thus, the proclamation of God's word connects us with the past, our biblical heritage, so that we can be changed now and live as hope-filled people. It also forces us to look forward.

The above-mentioned document also emphasizes the role of the Holy Spirit in the assembly as it hears that word. And so, although the gifts of the members are so different, and although each one hears the word at one's own "moment of history," unity is strengthened in the same Spirit. That unity, as well as the personal response of each worshiper, is expressed in the responsorial psalm. How hard that often is in practice! Sometimes the text is arbitrarily chosen by cantor or choir and has no reference to the theme of the reading. Psalms, too, are not always easy prayers for us. Nevertheless, this response should be one of the high points of the Mass for us. It should be our "yes" to the reading heard. One needs faith to hear God's word, but hearing that word also nurtures faith.

One of the finest changes since the Second Vatican Council has been the opportunity to hear God's word in our own langauge, so that it can do for us all which is described above. A lifetime of hearing that word and responding to it—that surely should make us different people, Christ-like people.

◆

The homily is an essential part of the liturgy, as it brings the Gospel message into our daily lives. It is one of those choice moments when life and liturgy meet. There is no doubt that such a moment places a heavy responsibility on the homilist. Should all the burden be on one person? Yet, a "committee" homily makes one shudder. What can the congregation do?

I would like to respond by mentioning one of the surprises I received when I first went to Rome to study in 1948. It came from student reactions during lectures. If the professor said something of special note or if he terminated a brilliant *tour de force* of reasoning (or of annihilation of an opponent), all the students stomped their feet on the wooden platform to which our desks were screwed. It is true that some professors played to the grandstands, and one could hear from such classrooms an almost continual pounding of feet. After class ended dust always hung in the air. Others, however, were more sober so that the occasional foot-pounding was genuine approval which was well merited. One finds similar reactions in black congregations. Here approval is shown by "Amens," "Alleluias" and other encouraging words. It is amazing how much better one preaches if such support is given.

The interplay between speaker and listener is important. Such reaction is like applause in the theater, the laughter which greets a well-said joke, the squeal which comes in the frightening scenes of a movie. No reaction makes one awkward and ill-at-ease.

During the four years I stayed at St. Malachy's Church on 49th Street and Broadway in New York, Fred Allen would always be in the front pew for the 11:15 Mass on Sunday morning. Even if a priest were to stand on his head, Fred would just glance up and give only that immovable, deadpan expression. It was difficult to preach and receive no sign of comprehension. Yet, after Mass, he would let the priest know he had been wide, wide awake and had caught every nuance.

I am sure, however, that most people do not realize how frustrating it is to get up in the pulpit and face a church full of expressionless faces. Often the faces even seem hostile. "Try to say anything I haven't heard before or that can move me," they seem to say. Most of the time they look tired. "Get it over with. Don't make it too long," they say, as they look at their watches, fiddle with the bulletin, continue to button and unbutton their sweaters. But there are always, thank God, a few faces which look up with eagerness, catch one's eye, and seem to say, "I am alert, eager to hear your message." These same eyes smile when something is said which appeals or hits home. One knows they are attentive and this is encouraging. It might not be the same as stomping feet, but it is the equivalent thereof.

If you want a good homily, prod the celebrant into it by your attentiveness and your reactions. If he says something "right on," don't be afraid to smile and shake your head affirmatively. If you look puzzled, he will clarify with a better expression; if you look troubled, disapproving, he may mollify his tone a bit.

There are many books written today on how to preach well. What we need, too, are some instructions on how to listen creatively and assist the priest with correct reactions. Even an occasional word of affirmation after Mass might help the celebrant know what was helpful and hit home.

◆

The prayers of intercession are also a choice moment when liturgy meets life. They begin, not with a prayer to God, but with a reminder to all of us of God's goodness and mercy. In that context we have the trust needed to make our petitions. The introduction is to encourage us, to help us to pour forth our needs.

But these petitions, coming as they do during the Eucharist, should be a link to the larger Church and the larger world and not just our own personal hurts. These hurts, however, should not be omitted, just seen in a larger context.

◆

Although the offertory procession should be short, not unduly elaborated and not central, and although the offertory itself should not be extended, the sentiments or attitudes which accompany them are most important. They do properly belong to the eucharistic prayer, as such, which follows. An offering is always a part of the prayer which follows the words of institution. The real offering takes place during the Eucharistic prayer or canon, but so much is going on there that this part is more or less anticipated so that we have more time to reflect.

How are we to offer ourselves and our lives with Christ?

When the document of Vatican II on the Church stated that Christ shares his priestly office with each baptized just as he shares his life and his mission, it stated a truth with tremendous personal consequences for our spiritual life. In baptism each Christian is anointed by the Holy Spirit so that the life of the Spirit can develop within each one. The growth of the life of the Spirit within us is really what spiritual life is all about. It means that everything we do—our daily work, our relaxation, our prayers, our good deeds, all our hardships, sufferings, and joys—can become a part of the sacrifice offered by Christ to his Father. For a time in the Church this was included in a kind of daily offering which the faithful were encouraged to make. This was not a new idea in the Church; it was only a clear recognition of a truth found already in the First Letter of St. Peter: "You too are living stones, built as an edifice of spirit, into a holy priesthood, offering spiritual sacrifices acceptable to God through Jesus Christ" (1 Pet 2:5).

The moment given us for such an offering of self and of one's whole life is at the offertory of the Mass. In that way they are offered in the celebration of the Eucharist to the Father along with the body of the Lord. The priest echoes this prayer of each person as he says quietly during the offertory: "Lord God, we ask you to receive us and be pleased with the sacrifice we offer you with humble and contrite hearts." So many of the prayers said over the gifts restate, often in almost matter-of-fact terms, this powerful concept.

The same Vatican document then, in a kind of visionary way, sees the faithful, the world over, offering themselves and their lives and their actions so that the world itself becomes consecrated to God.

For all of this to make sense to a Christian, one must recall the sacrificial nature of the Eucharist and its relationship to the offering of Jesus himself on Cavalry for the redemption of the world. At Mass we join ourselves to that same offering. We are able to do this because we share in Christ's priesthood. We are united, by baptism, to his death and resurrection. Thus, our own lives and work share in his redemptive power, his Calvary, his resurrection. These are not mere words. This is not just a pious thought. The Eucharist becomes a moment—a peak moment—when the Christian can be truly one with Christ in the offering of self and thus in the sanctification of this world. The document of Vatican II on the liturgy puts it this way (note how it states that *all* are involved): "Offering the Immaculate Victim, not only *through* the hands of the priest but also *together with him*, the faithful should learn to offer themselves" (#48).

For these reasons all our petitions, the collection, the rites of profession, ordination, confirmation, and so on, take place at the offertory. It becomes a short but intense moment of union with the suffering and risen Lord and a sign of the priesthood of the faithful: Christ indeed associates all of us in his work, in his mission. At the offertory we again say our "yes."

How does this offering affect our spirituality? How often we have heard people tell us when times are rough: "Offer it up." Is this what is involved?

If the idea behind the phrase is a kind of passive attitude that accepts whatever comes without trying to change one's lot or without resisting evil and fighting back, then, of course, the phrase is not really Christian. For a follower of Christ life is not just a series of painful events which one somehow submits to. Christianity is a positive attitude toward the whole of life and especially toward suffering and pain.

First of all, one will inevitably experience suffering and pain. No one escapes misfortunes and setbacks in life. There is no one without physical suffering and periods of anxiety and worry. There is no one who doesn't find himself or herself in circumstances which cannot be altered or changed. When the death of a loved one comes or when we are gravely sick, we must face up to such circumstances with realism.

What, then, is the Christian way of "offering it up"?

That way consists in joining our sufferings to those of Jesus on the cross. We become one with him in his moment of facing death. This attitude is not just being pious, but is grounded theologically. When we speak of the priesthood of the faithful that is the result of baptism, we mean that every—note, every!—baptized person can offer sacrifice with and in Christ. This is a real power. As St. Paul said to the Romans, we should offer ourselves to God as a living sacrifice. "And now, brothers and sisters, I beg you through the mercy of God to offer your bodies as a living sacrifice holy and acceptable to God, your spiritual worship" (Rom 12:1).

When is this offering of self most clearly effected? It is done at the Eucharist. Offering one's self at the Eucharist is not just a devotional custom; it is part of what Eucharist means. *Lumen Gentium* of Vatican II states: "The faithful join in the offering of the Eucharist by virtue of their royal priesthood" (par. 10). And, again, in the next paragraph one reads: "Taking part in the eucharistic sacrifice, which is the font and apex of the whole Christian life, they offer the divine Victim to God, and offer themselves along with it."

In the sacrament of anointing, too, this concept of union with the suffering Lord is also clear.

What is also evident in all of these texts is that the offering is not passive resignation or indifference, but a positive union with the suffering Christ to participate in his glory and resurrection. Thus, over the shadow of pain shines the purifying light of hope in redemption and resurrection. Only in this way is suffering redemptive and not oppressive. We offer up suffering and pain and misunderstanding—to the Father, with and in Jesus. Our suffering is then not blind fate or useless and wasted moments, but a part of God's plan of redemption begun on the cross. We will then realize that, just as our pain is his pain and our work is his work and our death is a sharing in his death, so his joy and triumph will be our joy and triumph. "Jesus, suffer in me and through me, and I can then offer it up to the Father under the sign of Eucharist, of thanksgiving, of victory."

◆

Eucharist means thanksgiving, saying thanks to God as we remember all he has done for us but especially for the death and resurrection of Jesus Christ, his Son, our Lord. I wonder, as we begin the preface and during the Eucharistic prayer, if all our hearts are full of gratitude. I wonder what most people think of at that moment. But it is the center of the spiritual life of the Church and there is so much to give thanks for.

The Eucharist is a memorial, a remembrance of Christ's dying and rising again, his ascension into glory, and also his sending of the Spirit. This memorial aspect, essential to the Eucharist, is called in Greek *anamnesis*. When Jesus was about to die, he gathered his closest followers around him and celebrated the paschal meal with them. He left them that symbolic meal as a memorial *(anamnesis)* of his passion, death, and resurrection. The oldest account of this event which has come down to us is found in St. Paul's First Letter to the Church at Corinth. In chapter 11 of that letter, he is rather harsh on the Corinthians because they did not understand what the implications of celebrating that memorial were for creating a community of love and sharing. He states that he was handing on what he had received, namely, "that the Lord Jesus on the night on which he was betrayed took bread, and after he had given thanks, broke it and said, 'This is my body, which is for you. *Do this in remembrance of me.*' In the same way, after the supper, he took the cup, saying, 'This cup is the new covenant in my blood. Do this, whenever you drink it, *in remembrance of me.*' Every time, then, you eat this bread and drink this cup, you proclaim the death of the Lord until he comes!"

One could say, thus, that the high point of the Mass is the eucharistic prayer offered by the presiding priest, in the name of the assembly, to the Father, and in that prayer it is the *anamnesis* which is indeed central. Some scholars include under the term *anamnesis* the whole institutional narrative quoted from St. Paul above and then the words immediately following the words of institution.

After the priest says, "Do this in remembrance of me," he says, "Let us proclaim this mystery of faith." This phrase historically has nothing to do with transubstantiation, but gives the people an opportunity to make their *anamnesis,* their remembrance. It is for this reason that the acclamations which follow remember the passion, death, and resurrection of Christ: "Dying you destroyed our death, rising you restored our life. Lord Jesus, come in glory." "Christ has died, Christ is risen, Christ will come again." "When we eat this bread and drink this cup, we proclaim your death,

Lord Jesus, until you come in glory." (Note that as people's prayers they are addressed to Jesus.) It is a shame that some do not know the meaning of this liturgical moment and sing almost anything.

The priest continues with the *anamnesis* prayer. In the first or Roman eucharistic prayer it is clear and complete: "Father, we celebrate the memory of Christ, your Son. We, your people and your ministers, recall his passion, his resurrection from the dead and his ascension into glory." Eucharistic prayer II: "In memory of his death and resurrection, we offer you, Father, etc." Eucharistic prayer III: "Father, calling to mind the death your Son endured for our salvation, his glorious resurrection and ascension into heaven, and ready to greet him when he comes again, etc." Eucharistic prayer IV: "Father, we now celebrate this memorial of our redemption. We recall Christ's death, his descent among the dead, his resurrection, and his ascension to your right hand, and, looking forward to his coming in glory, etc." Each time we are participating at Eucharist we hear these words—a reminder that what we are about is a remembrance and that through that symbolic memorial act the effects of the original event are made present to us.

God has indeed been good to us! No wonder the word Eucharist mean thanks!

♦

We should not forget that liturgy is made up of meaningful signs and symbols. Often we think that these signs can only be objects—water, fire, candles—but we should not forget that actions and interactions of people can also be signs. One of the most important action signs of the Mass is the rite of peace.

As with other signs, it is important that our interior disposition correspond with the content of the symbolic act. In other words, it is important that we know what we are doing and really mean it. First of all, we must remember that the sign of peace is and must remain a sign. In other words again, it says more than the external act itself might suggest. Let me give an example. If someone is talking and we agree with what that person is saying, we shake our head up and down. In such a case the shaking motion to us Americans says more than "I am shaking my head"—it says "I agree."

There are many other gestures and actions which in our culture are used as signs. Sometimes they become highly stylized, like tilting one's head to the side and resting it on one's hands to show sleep. Sometimes a sign may be ambiguous and mean several things; only the circumstances make it clear. For example, a football referee might roll his hands one over the other many times to show a penalty for a man in motion in the backfield and a crew on television might use the same sign to say the clock is running out.

Back to the sign of peace! In the United States we use a handshake most often for that sign. What should it mean in this case? First of all, it does not mean "hello." The Communion rite at Mass is no place to be saying "hello." We are not at a party where we are introducing people and greeting them. That should be done before Mass if it seems necessary. Nor is the rite of peace a place for wishing all kinds of sympathy, consolation, best wishes, or personal nosegays.

Let us examine what the content of the sign should be. The rite of peace is connected with the final words of the Our Father: "Forgive us our trespasses as we forgive those who trespass against us." It is a way of saying that I hold nothing against my brother or sister before I participate fully in the sacrifice. It is also a way of saying that I want to receive and accept my brother and sister in the same way and with the same love that I receive and accept Jesus. And it means even more than that: I wish peace to all my brothers and sisters, that peace namely which comes from the fullness of Jesus' life and love in another. I wish them peace because we will be united in the same fullness of life in Jesus. The person next to me represents at that moment all men and women. I must be reconciled to all in that one symbolic act. Formerly the priest began the rite of peace by kissing the altar which represented Christ. He then extended it to all in a kind of chain reaction. This sign made it clear that all were united in the same life of Jesus. That same intention and expression of unity is still present in our less complicated form.

As we shake hands with the person nearest us (and one is really enough for the symbolic act to be complete), we publicly seek reconciliation with all and wish them the fullness of Christian life. It might be only a handshake, but it is certainly packed with meaning.

◆

During the *fractio* or breaking of the bread the "Lamb of God" is sung. It should arouse within our minds and hearts a whole set of texts and passages in both the Old and the New Testaments.

"Lamb of God, you take away the sins of the world; have mercy on us." How often we say those words! Each day at Mass we repeat them as the host is being broken. Then the priest raises the host before Communion and says, "This is the Lamb of God who takes away the sins of the world. Happy are those who are called to his supper." It was John the Baptizer who first applied these words to Jesus. When John caught sight of Jesus coming toward him in the desert, he said, "Look, there is the Lamb of God who takes away the sin of the world" (Jn 1:29).

On hearing that title, the devout Jew at the time of Jesus would have been reminded of many texts in the Scriptures.

First of all, he would have remembered the description of the suffering servant described in Isaiah 53—dying, this servant would pay for the sins of his people; he appeared as a lamb led to the slaughter, like a sheep before the shearers, silent and not opening his mouth. This was the same passage, if you recall, that the Ethiopian eunuch was reading in Acts 8 when Philip overtook him on the road south from Jerusalem to Gaza. Philip explained how Jesus was this lamb. Jesus kept silent before the Sanhedrin; he answered nothing to Pilate. He will bear our guilt, he will surrender himself to death to win pardon for our offenses.

But the image would have evoked even more to the devout Jew. He would have thought of those passages which related the story of the deliverance of his captive people from the slavery of Egypt. Each family of the Hebrews was to slaughter a lamb "without blemish," male, one year old (Ex 12), and mark the lintels of the door with its blood. The exterminating angel thus passed by and spared those families. "Saved by the blood of the lamb" meant loved by God, protected by God, and freed from slavery. It meant they were able to become a consecrated nation, a kingdom of priests. They were to be bound to God by a covenant—the covenant being sealed by blood.

No wonder, then, that Peter, and John in particular, point out that Jesus is the lamb without blemish, without sin, who delivers us at the price of his blood. Thanks to the blood of this lamb, Christ, a new covenant was formed, making all baptized into a royal priesthood, a consecrated nation. At the consecration of each Mass we repeat that the wine changed into Christ's blood is the blood of the new covenant, shed for all people, so that sins may be forgiven.

St. Paul, writing to Corinth, could remind the Christians to live as if on unleavened bread, because "Christ, our pasch, has been immolated" (1 Cor 5:7). In the passion narrative by St. John, Jesus is put to death the night before the feast of unleavened bread—thus, the day of the pasch, in the afternoon, at the very hour when, according to the prescriptions of the law, the lambs were being immolated in the temple. John also reminds us that the prescription for the passover meal given in Exodus 12:46 mentions that the bones of the lamb should not be broken; so the soldiers do not break Jesus' bones.

Lamb thus means meekness, innocence, but also nourishment. The blood of the lamb means freedom from sin and slavery. It means sacrifice and redemption. It means forgiveness. It means new covenant, a new people.

But the story of the paschal lamb would not be complete without the visions of the Book of Revelation. After the resurrection there is a new hymn in heaven: "Worthy is the Lamb that was slain to receive power and riches, wisdom and strength, honor and glory and praise" (Rev 5:12). Revelation ends in chapter 22 with a vision of the river of life-giving water issuing from the throne of God and of the lamb. There all will be fertile and fruitful. Night will be no more. From there Jesus says: "Remember, I am coming soon."

◆

Now, I have a confession to make. The one aspect of the liturgical reform which I feel has been misunderstood and which bothers me is the lack of time and atmosphere for personal prayer and reflection after Communion.

In describing the different elements of the Mass, the Introduction to the *New Roman Missal* mentions in paragraph 23 that "after Communion, all praise God in silent prayer." Somehow, however, this seems to get lost in the next section which deals with each part of the Mass, in particular. When the instruction treats of the Communion, it states that a Communion song should be sung to express outwardly the unity of all the believers, to give evidence of their joy, and to make the procession to receive the body and blood of Christ a community act. This same paragraph also mentions the possibility of a hymn after Communion sung by all. There is no mention of the possibility of a read meditation that becomes a kind of second homily or of other kinds of solo performances that abound today. It does state—perhaps too cautiously compared to what had been written earlier—that "after Communion, the priest and people may spend some time in silent prayer." It is a shame that this is not made a bit stronger.

One of the prime considerations affecting the renewal of the liturgy was the felt need to weed out all those excessive accretions which had overlaid the basic form of the Mass until it became almost unrecognizable. Now we seem to be constantly adding new things so that we might soon be back where we started from.

It is hard for people to remain silent for long and to simply pray from the bottom of their hearts. But many complain that the new liturgy does not give them time for personal prayer. This moment after Communion is meant as a remedy for just such a complaint. It is the *moment* for silent prayer.

The Communion rite ends, then, with the prayer which the priest recites, a prayer which petitions God to make effective in the lives of the participants the full depth and meaning of the sacrament received. It is thus not prudent to insert before that prayer all kinds of other acts, such as giving out diplomas and awards, announcements, and the like. The prayer does not end the Mass; it ends the Communion rite.

The difficulty with the rite of Communion is that it is both a very personal as well as a communal event. The liturgy, as a rule, presupposes the personal intention and, of its nature, tends to be a communal act. Nevertheless, the rite of Communion permits the personal to stand alone for a moment, so that the impact of the event can be more fully grasped. The union of the individual with Christ seems to demand silence, a pause for wonder and awe before continuing on to the communal implication that all have received of the *one* body and have drunk of the *one* cup.

I find I appreciate also that moment of silence after Communion because, so often, one cannot just pray when Mass is over. It seems that so many distractions occur then. This is especially true if the celebrant goes to the door of the church to greet people. Sometimes that moment of silence after Communion is all one has for personal thanksgiving. Let's make the most of it!

◆

How difficult it is to know how to end the Mass! It must, of course, lead to life. But participation in that act should also bring new light, new meaning, new fervor to our daily joys and sufferings. It is both an end and a beginning. It never ends the same, since our lives each time must bring the mystery of the Eucharist into a new moment of our own and the world's history. Perhaps that is also why the Eucharist is never the same for us but each repetition has a new meaning.

We never tire of the same, since it is always different.

Seasonal Reflections

Just as we have walked through the Eucharist, so now we should briefly glance at the liturgical year. That cycle does not change the Mass as Mass but it does add a significant means of probing more deeply into the mystery of the Christ-event which is celebrated at each Eucharist.

In what follows more attention is given to Christmas than to Advent itself. There are so many aids for entering into the spirit of Advent—and we have four weeks in which to do so—but so little for Christmas itself. That feast often passes swiftly and we seldom reflect on its more personal meaning. Our guide through the Advent season is Mary.

If Advent and Christmas seem to bring us into a spiritual moment when the larger vision dominates, where we are swept up in history and see ourselves as a part of the larger mystery, Lent does just the opposite. Lent makes us see our fragility in its most disturbing way. Lent means that we acknowledge our "dustness" and our need for constant renewal.

My reflections center around the spirituality of these two major liturgical seasons—Advent and Lent/or Christmas and Easter—and our spiritual journey that is a part of such celebrations.

Advent/Christmas

The Advent season is Mary's season. It is not by coincidence that she plays such an important role in our own preparation for Christmas and in the celebration of the feast itself.

First of all, a word is in order about Mary and our own preparation for Christmas. The whole of the liturgical year presents the life of Christ squashed into 365 days. There was originally no attempt made to keep to a clear chronological or time sequence among the feasts; all events were telescoped into one year. Advent was the time of preparation for the birth of Christ and, thus, the annunciation was celebrated during Advent, not nine months before Christmas

in March. However, we still have a chance in Advent to meditate on Mary's role because of the feasts of the Immaculate
Conception and of Our Lady of Guadalupe. The feast of the
Immaculate Conception makes us aware of God's loving
care for all of us who are to be receiving his Son into our
lives. God's preparation of Mary to be the Mother of Jesus
reminds us in Advent of the need for our own preparedness.

In 1981 the members of our Church of Mexican origin
also celebrated the 450th anniversary of Our Lady of Guadalupe. On December 12, 1531, the poor Indian convert,
Juan Diego, received from Mary the roses, as he told the
story, which became imprinted on his cloak and transformed
into the famous image we all know. This story, like the one
of the visions of Lourdes, has both a theological and a pastoral importance, because such stories bring out the theme
of God's special love for the poor and the lowly. Mary herself echoed this theme of nothingness in her own prayer,
and it has since been called to our attention again in these
more popular events. The message on this anniversary of
Guadalupe was that God loves the poor in a very special way
and is at home with the unpretentious and the unsophisti-
cated, with those who are child-like. For this reason Jesus
was born of Mary, a poor, unknown Jewish girl. Mary, in
turn, becomes a source of encouragement to all of us.

On Christmas, if we feel "poor," helpless, and without
great visions and dreams, if we feel our creatureliness and
vulnerability, then we are ready to approach the crib with
trust and confidence. He wants to come into our lives in a
new Advent of love at Christmas.

Certain events in our lives change their whole direction.
We all can point out such moments and their effects. For
married couples it is undoubtedly the day they said their yes.
What priest cannot remember clearly his ordination day!
There are other events, less striking perhaps, but also mem-

orable because they marked a new moment—the first day of school and saying goodbye to the parent who brought us there, wearing long trousers for the first time, the first date and dance, graduations, and some birthdays. There are other events which have affected the whole life and history of this nation and the world. Everyone in a certain age bracket can tell you what he or she was doing when the Japanese struck at Pearl Harbor, when President Kennedy was shot.

There is one event which changed the history of the world and still changes the personal life of each of us. When God took on human flesh and became one of us, that incarnation altered the course of our communal and personal history. The thought of that event is in itself overwhelming: God is among us! Jesus is the fullest revelation of the Father. His birth opens up whole new vistas for us and for the human race. This would be enough, but the event is more than just a new divine presence in our midst. He came that we might share in his divine life! Such a thought just makes us stand still in awe. Could there be a God who loves us so much that he not only comes among us but he also wishes to share his life with us!

It seems that when one writes about the full meaning of Christmas one has to end every sentence with an exclamation point because of one's amazement and wonder. Indeed, that is the first aspect of Christmas. We are invited to look on that infant in the crib with wonder and awe. Christmas has a very important contemplative dimension and it should not be wanting.

But that event also changes our personal lives. In baptism we put on Christ. As we marvel at that infant in the manger, we see him proclaiming the good news, teaching and healing. We see him rejected. We see him suffering and dying for our sakes. We see him rising again from the dead.

We anticipate his return in glory. Thus, as we gaze on that babe, we see that our own life gets caught up in a new dynamic because we are with him. As his disciples, a new kind of life opens up for us, a new destiny awaits us. Our wonder and contemplation then lead to a new way of being human—one which does not lose its supernatural thrust. We become followers of the one we gaze on. We share in his life, in his mission, in his destiny. We are one with him. Christmas means that God is among us and that we can be with him. It will have importance only if we seek to receive him totally and permit that event to change us, to make us more and more Christ-like.

All good things in life are delicate, fragile, perishable. That is because the human element, of its nature, is mortal and will change and pass away. Yet in the moment of greatest weakness there often is a hint of hidden strength, of transcendent beauty, of lasting value. Christmas is such an event.

I used to think it was immature and un-Christian to let oneself become sentimental at Christmastime. But now I have changed my mind. There is no life without sentiment; there are special moments in life when sentiment is so much more meaningful than logic. Christmas is such a moment.

People are different at Christmastime. They seem to put the best side of their personality in evidence; their hidden lovable qualities seem to dominate. There is no place for the Scrooge in us! Why not be happy and rejoice at such sharing and accept it as a gift?

But Christmas is not a time for big melodramatic sweeps: the birth of a baby is too intimate for that kind of sentiment! Perhaps because we are waiting to be overwhelmed we miss the beauty of the smaller display of love and affection—no less real—that marks the Christmas season. The liturgy of the season begins by showing us a dark world, but a world full of hope and trust in God's goodness and loving forgiveness. Darkness covered the earth, so the prophet said. Into that darkness is born a child, a light, a flicker of new joy, a ray of hope fulfilled—most of all, a flame that cannot be extinguished, that cannot go out, that does not depend on human perishable sources of energy. That light is able, especially at Christmas, to cast its warmth and brightness on so many beautiful human objects which normally seem dull and bereft of feeling to us. It is also able to light up, in a contagious way, so many other, more earthly, lamps which are yearning for life. The trouble with all of us is that we are unable to absorb much genuine love and sentiment without it becoming maudlin. In our cumbersome way we seem to be able to snuff out with apparent ease the frail, short-wicked candles of human origin which surround us. If only we could see that God speaks to us through all those little flickers of light at Christmas. If only, somehow, we could capture them (like fireflies in a jar) and preserve them throughout the year.

What do you do with Christmas cards? I read them all as they come in before the feast but they are too much to assimilate. There are too many greetings from too many loved ones to absorb all that genuine, sincere well-wishing. I throw them in a box and toward the end of January take them out on a lazy day and read them slowly. Like good wine, those sentiments grow better with age. But it is also important to reflect on the transcendent source of all light and hope during the Christmas season. God's presence fills that Child; therefore, it is unquenchable light which is being shared, a light which cannot go out. During the year, when we seem again so often immersed in darkness, faith in that light will balance our sense of being overwhelmed by the perishable, fragile, human world around us.

Lent/Easter

Renewal is never too late. Nor is there an ideal place to begin the process of being renewed. One can enter at almost any level or stage. Renewal is like a many-layered object that remains a single unit but must be taken apart for our own study because the whole is too complicated and too profound to be grasped at once. Former stages are never abandoned but must always be made deeper.

Thus, in the Lenten period we hear again God's call to holiness, and we must again respond. We must be converted. Conversion does not happen once and for all, but is a daily affair. Lent, in a particular way, can help us hear again the call to be different people, faith-filled people, baptized people. Lent is also a good moment, a grace-filled moment, for renewing our discipleship. We say "yes" to following Christ at all costs; we say "yes" to the sacrifices and renunciations which accepting the cross demands.

But in the Lenten season we deal with the energizing role of the Holy Spirit in a special way. We must, as baptized and confirmed believers, become aware of the power of the Holy Spirit in our midst. There are various ways of looking at this role of the Spirit among us. (We must be careful not to limit the Spirit or seek to contain that Spirit in our own categories and pre-conceived notions.)

First of all, the Spirit is Jesus' gift to his people, to his Church. It was truly his last will and testament. Because it is his gift, it helps us to be more like him, more united to him. At confirmation the bishop prays that the gifts of the Spirit will make the newly-confirmed more like Christ. Thus the first function of the Spirit is to sanctify or make holy. That means that our baptismal insertion into the life of Christ becomes more real and more realized in our lives.

We also know that the Spirit is operative in a special way in the sacraments of the Church. The Spirit empowers us, makes us holy, through that sacramental participation. In the Eucharist, in particular, the power of the Spirit is evident, not only to make the gifts of bread and wine "holy" (transformed into the body and blood of Christ), but also, through our reception of this sacrament, to make us holy. How often in the Eucharist we allude to the power of the Spirit to make us one, to unite us all in the one Christ! Another aspect of the power of the Spirit, thus, is uniting. The Spirit does not nullify differences—on the contrary. St. Paul sees the source of all the different gifts as the one and same Spirit. For this reason it is so important that all see the need to participate as Church in the sacraments. It is there that the one Spirit brings us into unity and makes our gifts truly complementary. Only after this solid interior transformation, as members of a eucharistic community which is united and brought together by one and the same Spirit, can we see ourselves empowered to go forth and "renew the face of the earth."

Lent is indeed a good time to enter into that renewal of the Holy Spirit in our personal lives and as members of Church—that kind of sacramental renewal which leads to holiness and unity, so that we can be "sent" by the Spirit, missioned by the Spirit to spread the good news to others.

People who give up smoking tell me that they have the sensation of tasting for the first time. They realize that their taste buds had been dulled as suddenly they acquire a whole new attitude toward food and their daily eating habits. Lent and its penitential practices should do the same thing for us in the spiritual field. Lent should help us get down again to the basics of life and permit us to start over. We should be able at that time to see ourselves and our lives with a different attitude. Just as fasting, after having eaten too much rich food, makes the taste buds more sensitive, so our attitude toward life should be renewed by the discipline of Lent. Lent should help us see the ordinary things of life under a new perspective. In some cases we will see Christ for the first time in so many of the ordinary moments of life. Our spiritual sensitivity will be heightened. Christ is so often neglected in our daily routine because we have been accustomed to too much and we have neglected the ordinary. Or perhaps sin and bad habits, like smoking to the taste, have simply dulled our spiritual awareness. Lent helps us get back again to the importance of all the ordinary moments of our existence. It helps us to see how Jesus reveals himself in the day-by-day routine.

Lent helps us see Jesus in our moments of anxiety and concern. God's providence is always before our eyes. We find Jesus in our moments of joy and contentment. We see all our crosses as a part of the whole cycle of dying and rising, and thus resurrection and redemption are never absent from view. Lent helps us purify our love. We find Jesus in the selfless love we share with others and receive from them. The discipline of Lent helps us to be sensitive to those little experiences of mutual concern and support. Lent also helps us in admitting our helplessness. We fear being or becoming dependent; but Lent forces us to see that Jesus was helpless. We know, too, that we are never alone but always a part of a people whom God loves.

Lent clears away the smallness which comes from bogging down in details and helps us keep a larger vision of life; it makes us come to grips with what "success" really means. We do not become trapped in the quest for material gain. Lent also makes us more sensitive to the beauty around us. As winter passes into spring we become more attuned to the subtle changes of nature and rejoice in her groanings to bring forth new life.

The discipline of Lent, then, should make us more alert, more awake, more alive. It should heighten our sense of hearing, listening, responding, seeing, watching, waiting. Little things should mean more to us because our dulled spiritual taste buds have come again to life. Lent lets faith penetrate our daily existence and the ordinary of each day becomes full of the presence of the risen Lord. Life is renewed. No wonder St. Benedict said that a monk's life should be a perpetual Lent!

In chapter 58 of the prophet Isaiah, we read what true fasting is all about. The Lord rejects fasting which does not result in a new attitude toward others. "This, rather, is the fasting that I wish: releasing those bound unjustly, untying the thongs of the yoke; setting free the oppressed, breaking every yoke, sharing our bread with the hungry, sheltering the oppressed and the homeless; clothing the naked when you see them, and not turning your back on your own" (Is 58:6–7). Fasting according to this passage of Isaiah is not just inner purification that results in a conquest of passion, but it must lead to sharing with others. In this respect fasting for a Christian is totally different in motivation and objective than dieting for health reasons, or mortifying the body for penance, or controlling the appetite for a kind of nirvana. Fasting curbs egotism and helps control all one's appetites, but this done for the sake of our neighbor. The Fathers of the Church saw the results of fasting to be almsgiving, that is, what we deprived ourselves of was given to another.

It is true that fasting was seen as a kind of freeing and liberating process, making mind and heart (and body) a bit lighter, helping to make us more sensitive to the movement of the Spirit. But wealth was not piled up: fasting did not make one richer, fasting did not accumulate for later surfeiting. Fasting had a social dimension: almsgiving. It became a kind of leveling process between rich and poor. A bond of consciousness of human weakness must result. It was to become a sign of solidarity with the "permanently fasting"—the poor and needy.

Almsgiving implies also the spiritual and not just the corporal works of mercy. There is a concern about all captive people and those who hunger and thirst for justice. As one becomes freer and more liberated through fasting from earthly necessities, one sees how those held in any bondage are our brothers and sisters, who must also be freed.

Prayer, fasting, and almsgiving have always belonged together as a part of Christian asceticism. Fasting liberates and heightens one's sense of dependence on God and the need to free oneself from false securities. Fasting heightens one's sense of solidarity with all human beings in their weakness and "earthliness" and points out the need to share. Fasting leads inevitably, then, to heightened prayer. Dependence on God becomes the source of deeper union with him. The Spirit can breathe more freely. But it also leads to a deeper communal prayer, as one senses a deeper union with every other person: sharing of goods is not enough; all needs of our brothers and sisters become our own and are felt more deeply.

If you have this kind of fasting, Isaiah explains, "Then the Lord will guide you always and give you plenty even on the parched land. He will renew your strength, and you shall be like a watered garden, like a spring whose water never fails" (Is 58:11).

Lent, too, always forces us again to face up to the mystery of suffering. We know, in faith, that suffering can be redemptive, if only we can find a way of uniting ourselves with Jesus in his own passion and death. Our faith tells us that our trials and hurts are not in vain. We cannot void them if we want to live fully, and thus there must be a positive and redeeming feature about them. The example I would like to point out in the Lenten season also is Mary. So often her sufferings are brought to our attention and might help us in analyzing and making sense out of our own situation. Mary suffered because she was so closely united to Jesus in love and affection as well as by parental bond. Her suffering was not the martyr's physical endurance test, but that of the one in love seeing the loved one suffer. To stand helplessly by and see another whom one loves suffer—senselessly and unjustly—is the deepest kind of suffering. We call that "compassion"—to suffer with another. The Church sees its model in Mary. Thus we, as Christians, also have something to learn from Mary about what compassion and suffering mean.

First of all, we must learn, all of us, that being united in affection and love with Jesus is the basis of Christian discipleship. Because of that union we can have compassion when we meditate on his sufferings and death. Like Mary, we stand helplessly by.

One should, however, go one step further in this understanding of Mary's love and, thus, of her compassion. We know that Jesus accepted his cross and death because of his love for us. He had compassion on us. He identified, in love, with our human suffering and took it upon himself. So, if we are one with him in love and affection, we must also be one with every one of our suffering brothers and sisters whom he loves. Love of him, compassion on his sufferings, implies love of those he loves and compassion on their sufferings.

Mary, we know, became at that moment of his suffering our Mother. Jesus, dying, presented her to us. She is the model, then, of one who is united to our suffering as she was to her Son's. She is united to all whom he loves.

If Mary is the model of the Church, then what kind of Church must we be? Without doubt—a compassionate one. Redemptive love is possible if we are united with the Redeemer. All of his suffering led to resurrection and the triumph of life over death. One with him in suffering (compassion) leads to one with him in resurrection. Jesus loved us so much as to suffer death for us. Mary, because she loved him so, suffered to see him suffer. She became our Mother and suffers, in love, for and with us. As model of the Church, she thus teaches us to be united, in our suffering, to Jesus in his suffering and in this way to all of those he loves. United with him in suffering we will be united with him in resurrection. A compassionate Church is a redeemed and loving Church.

STRESS POINTS

Part IV

The Church in the Modern World: Stress Points

After the bishops at the Second Vatican Council had drafted a document on the nature of the Church (*Lumen Gentium*), they felt a certain sense of incompleteness in their work. Led by Cardinals Montini (later to become Pope Paul VI) and Suenens, they began a new document on the relationship between the Church and the world at this given moment of history (*Gaudium et Spes*), the *Pastoral Constitution on the Church in the Modern World.* In a sense this second document has never been, and will never be, fully worked out, since times continue to change. Nevertheless, we must mention that one pastoral problem was present from the earliest moments of the Church's history and has continued to be a part of the life of the Church to our day. Perhaps one could describe this perennial tension as the challenge to the unity of the Church which comes from inner and external growth, from contact with new situations and new cultures. It is the age-old question of growth with unity and continuity. Strains on the Church's unity are always easier to handle if they can be brought out in the open to be dealt with in honest and sincere struggle. Analyzing them helps to find solutions. The apostles found that out at the First Council of Jerusalem!

Some of the stresses are internal, that is, they affect the inner cohesiveness of the members of the Church because they stem from differing theologies, or, as one says today, differing ecclesiologies. Some of these inner tensions come from the old question of how much pluralism a community can tolerate and not fall apart because of a lack of coherent, mutually accepted beliefs. Almost all inner tensions come from this need to delineate the territory within which a healthy pluralism can be acceptable and the limits beyond which such pluralism becomes divisive and destructive of the whole. Sometimes the tensions are aggravated by the lack of forums for discussion and analysis, more than from the ideas themselves. We Americans are especially sensitive to the lack of those processes which are needed for clear dialogue and we sense frustration when we are not able to grapple with an issue openly. Some areas of tension and stress are thus particular to each nation or section of the world; some are felt as a part of the universal Church.

It would be helpful to discuss, for example, those tensions peculiar to the Church in the United States today. Many of them revolve around the issue of separation of Church and state, of the speaking out of the Church on political issues with moral implications, and of the working out of the ramifications of the whole document on religious liberty of the Second Vatican Council in our democratic society. These questions have special import today in the light of the American bishops' pastoral letter on the question of nuclear weapons in the whole context of war and peace. On the flip side of the coin has been the rise of a kind of new "nativism," a new fear of Catholic power or influence on the U.S. scene. It has posed new tensions for the Church.

One could add to this new role of the Church on the domestic scene the statements of the American bishops which have also involved them in U.S. policies outside the United States—the statements on Central America and Lebanon, for example. The same questions arise among religious because of their missionary involvement in third world nations. The study of the U.S. economy in the light of Catholic social teaching is also a case where the Church looks at society and makes reflections that have necessary, almost built-in tensions.

There is another whole set of tensions which affect the inner life of a Church that has grown and expanded to every culture of the globe and that continues to seek its unity and continuity through a highly centralized system of control. One should not be hesitant to deny the existence of areas of concern in the relationship between, on the one hand, such a large and powerful nation and Church as that found in the United States, with its history of phenomenal growth in a pluralistic, democratic nation, and its bond to Rome, on the other.

Such a large expansion of the Church into so many cultures, the emphasis on collegiality in the documents of Vatican II, and the rise of national and regional conferences of bishops have posed new questions concerning the authority and levels of teaching within the Church itself. Even in the particular dioceses and on the parish level new consultative pastoral bodies have brought forth a dynamic of shared leadership and questioning of roles that create a different kind of functioning for Church structures.

On a global level serious concerns have arisen to challenge the Church as never before. Some call these areas the Church's new "Galileo." Perhaps no three stand out as much as the questions of nuclear weapons and world peace, the role of women in society and Church, and the whole network of questions which rise out of human sexuality. The Church in these last two sets of issues finds itself in the middle of gigantic cultural upheavals and unfinished scientific investigations. It has made, indeed, a brave beginning in the first set. The last two, however, have not seen much progress or insight.

In this section I would like to reflect on these areas of stress and tension as the Church faces not just a modern world, but the new challenges which this specific age brings.

They will set its agenda till we reach the end of the millennium.

Because the problem is not new but inherent in the very nature of the Church as "catholic" or trans-cultural, it would be helpful to begin with some reflections on the question as found at the very beginning of the Church's history before looking at our present-day versions of the same.

Learning from History

In scanning the New Testament, one finds the problem of unity and diversity experienced everywhere. To solve the tension it is not enough to quote the enticing description of the Church by St. Paul in his Epistles to the Romans and the Corinthians. There he points to the diversity of gifts as coming from the one same Spirit, all of them mutually complementary and thus operative in building up the body of Christ. Unity, too, he understands as coming from that same Spirit. But we all know too well that diametrically opposing factors often cite the same Spirit as their source. We superiors have all had to deal with people who claimed they were called by the Spirit to actions of a quite dubious nature, if not contrary to the Gospel. Ontologically one can explain unity as the result of action based on the same Spirit, but in existential reality the action of the Spirit must first be discerned as such, often with struggle and extensive prayer.

The picture of multiple gifts must also, *pro dolor,* be balanced by the acceptance of our own sinfulness and need for conversion. We could call it multiple sinfulness. One should not assume that all divisions come from well-meaning people with divergent ideas. The reality of sin is also present and divides. Of these sins certainly pride and selfishness are at the top of the list. In so many of Paul's letters he points out the errors which come from pride. We, too, must be aware of the fact that divisions in a community can come from sinfulness, especially from pride and egoism. Jesus warned his disciples of those wicked designs that well up from the deep recesses of the heart and that divide: acts of fornication, theft, murder, adulterous conduct, greed, maliciousness, deceit, sensuality, envy, blasphemy, arrogance, and obtuse spirit (Mk 7:21–22).

Sin is indeed divisive; selfishness and desire for personal aggrandizement are never wanting. The constant animosities which one finds in the Gospels toward Jesus that ultimately led to his death are a reality. At times one senses underneath them the fears of change, of the loss of the status quo and of religious power. Jesus knew that his teaching and person would bring division into families and society. We would be naive not to expect such motivation in our midst today. It is well for all of us to remember this fact, lest we ascribe all division to purely intellectual or rational approaches to challenges and problems. These passages are also good reminders to us and force us to look into our own hearts.

Nevertheless, it is helpful to reflect on the early Church from the standpoint of new tensions which followed immediately after the death of Jesus and which came from preaching the Gospel outside of Jewish culture.

One of the finest biblical scholars whom I had the privilege of knowing and of listening to with frequency in the 1970's was Jacques Dupont, O.S.B. The Acts of the Apostles was the object of his lifelong study and concern. Often I heard him say that the upheavals of those first generations of Christians had special import for the Church today, because the same questions were being asked then—questions which, I judge, each period of cultural change must face but each within its own peculiar historical framework.

First of all, identity was a problem for the nascent Church. On one hand, those early Christians struggled to keep in touch with their Jewish roots, even though the rift between Synagogue and Church grew larger and larger. On the other, they continued to grow in the midst of a pagan, Hellenistic world, taking what was good and integrating it in their lives, leaving the dross behind. Conversion and its consequences for lifestyle demanded constantly renewed reflection. Were those descriptions of "having all things in common" to be taken literally or were they models, examples, of needed charity? What about all those strange manifestations of the Spirit, "tongues and charisms"? What did persecution really mean to a beginning Church? How were the Scriptures fulfilled in Jesus? Most of all, how could the Church be open to the Gentiles and not be a divided Church, some members following Jewish customs, some not? Large distances between communities must have posed an almost insurmountable problem for Church unity, thus making Paul's trips important moments for again establishing continuity. His letters hint at constant problems which arose from lack of contact and communication. One of the benefits, thus, from reading Acts is that we sense our own day then is not unique.

Perhaps, though, no chapter in Acts is so revealing as chapter 15 which describes the First Council of Jerusalem. (Paul refers to that meeting again in Galatians 2.) The problem of the observance of Jewish ritual was an enormous one, capable of dividing the new Church into many antagonistic factions. Paul made his way—with witnesses—up to Jerusalem to discuss his experience among the Gentiles, to outline how the Spirit had been working in the Churches he had founded. It was an important meeting, not for debating, but for discerning the action of the Spirit among the faithful. Peter, too, began with experiences of the action of the Spirit among the Gentiles (the case of Cornelius and his family) and thus corroborated the position of Paul. (This was the second time Paul felt a need to go up to Jerusalem to consult the heads of the Church there.)

How today does one "go up to Jerusalem" to discuss experiences of the workings of the Spirit among us and discern that action of the Spirit in the midst of God's people?

There is no doubt that subsequent generations attempted to do so by also holding Church councils. Local councils became very common in the early Church and were held to discuss important and weighty matters. General councils were held for very urgent problems. Today we bishops meet on a provincial level, regional level, and national level. These meetings take time but they are precious moments of discernment—limited, as they are, in time, scope, import, and membership. On the universal level such encounters are rare, and the lack thereof is indeed a concern among many. After the Second Vatican Council it was the hope of many that the synods of bishops, as suggested by the council, would become the much-needed ongoing vehicle for such dialogue. Unfortunately that simply has not taken place. These meetings are held every three years with a very limited agenda and, for lack of time and clarity of procedures, seldom come to inspiring conclusions. But indeed they are something.

Pope John Paul II must also be struggling with these needs; his long and fatiguing trips to local Churches all over the world remind us of the early ones of St. Paul. Even what seemed a resurrection of an anachronistic institution such as the college of cardinals as an advisory body might be such an attempt to find an answer, though many Americans, perhaps overly sensitive to the freedom, openness, effectiveness, and representative character of such processes, comment that they do not find a totally-appointed body the best means for hearing the truth. But still it is something. Everyone knows that the Church was not established as a democracy. It is a peculiar type of monarchy, one in which all the faithful—including Popes and bishops—are guided by the same Spirit, follow the same Gospel, and seek the same Kingdom of God. Thus there is need to listen to the action of the Spirit as it is manifested in all the members of the Church. Vehicles for such listening processes on an international level are now lacking. For this reason sometimes, because the hurt has not been carefully diagnosed, the solutions proposed are not the right ones. At other times, valid, creative insights and contributions from one nation or group are passed by because there is no vehicle for their communication to the larger Church.

I would say that the group which suffers most in the United States from such a vacuum at this moment is women and especially women religious. Having taken seriously the vision of Church outlined in Vatican II and having struggled to listen to one another and the Church where they live and work, religious women, in particular, sense a void in communicating now to higher authorities where they are in their faith-journey. Such frustrations can only lead to sorrow and distrust. How can they—and so many others who are hurting—"go up to Jerusalem" today?

Because the Church has grown much larger, there is even more need for clearer channels of communication. There is undoubtedly more need also for more mutual trust and subsidiarity. The possibility of dealing with all aspects of credal expression in all cultures by one single office becomes unimaginable. Human limitations prevent accuracy and thoroughness. When the problems are internal to a nation, that is, when they stem from the long history of the way a Church relates to the political power within a nation, in these cases the local or regional Church must exercise its own collegial authority and sort out the questions facing it and proportionate answers.

The Church in the United States Today

Many today feel that there is a resurgence of anti-Catholicism in the nation. Is it true? If so, what are its roots? First of all, I think that one can dismiss as of no consequence such wild statements as those of evangelist Jimmy Swaggert who recently stated that the Catholic Church is a religion of "ignorance, superstition, and sin." Several other fundamentalist groups hold similar views; but these, too, come more from a lack of knowledge than from serious reasoning. In addition, the large number of novels on the best-seller list and a spate of Broadway plays, movies, and TV scripts which seem to point out the seamier side of Catholic life do not, it seems to me, reflect anti-Catholic biases as much as personal hurts as well as ambivalent fascinations with the Church and life within the Church.

What is of more concern is the return of older and deeper biases—those which held that Catholicism cannot be reconciled with the whole of the tenets of American democracy and remains a threat to it. Even to some of our founding fathers, such as Thomas Jefferson, there appeared a basic incompatibility between Catholicism and the principles of the Enlightenment expressed in the Constitution. It is not surprising that seven of the thirteen original colonies continued to carry some kind of anti-Catholic legislation after the Bill of Rights. The bitter religious controversies of the early 1800's which led up to the Know-Nothing Movement by now should have been long forgotten, even if they seemed to emerge about every quarter century in our history since then. Everyone felt that they died forever with the election of President Kennedy.

The general term used to describe the conflict between the democratic and Protestant principles upon which the nation was founded and Catholicism is usually called "nativism." Fear that the immigrants would take jobs from the working class or bring into the melting pot of the United States undesirable "lower-class" qualities was probably as strong in the mix as purely religious considerations. Most of the charges against the Church centered on the fear that the Church was an international power, closed to the advances of modern scientific research, and also closed to the kind of compromise that the pluralistic U.S. society was based on. There arose the fear that the large number of immigrants, voting *en bloc* with orders from the clergy and Rome, would control the political scene.

Why have these fears risen again in our day? Certainly the pastoral letter of the U.S. Conference of Bishops on the morality of the use of nuclear weapons is a sign that the Church is entering into public debate on a political issue. This has awakened new fears. The Church's stance on abortion and its support for anti-abortion legislation have made some others uneasy. Probably, too, the powerful influence of Pope John Paul II on the world scene has again attracted notice to the Church as a force in the social fabric of the world—one not to be ignored. The Church is speaking out now on many issues, but what the Church is saying is not new. It has been making statements in the United States for some sixty years now. Suddenly, however, these statements have assumed a new importance, bringing to the society a debate on moral values, speaking to issues at the heart of the nation's well-being. Perhaps some of the blame for the revival of nativist arguments comes from our own hesitancy and inability to articulate where we are in the political discourse. There should be no fear that Catholics want to form a political party of their own. There should be no fear that all Catholics will vote the same way on any given issue. Experience itself and knowledge should dissipate such fears. Nevertheless, there is a suspicion that the Church has shown from its history that it is intolerant of other views, and that the whole of society must march to its moral tune.

If, a few years back, you had stopped people on the street and asked what the position of the Catholic Church was on the relationship between Church and state, they might have responded with the following as a kind of uninformed, but typical, view: The Church would want to be the official religion of the state with a special status: other religions would be tolerated if they were not too dangerous to the unity of the nation.

There is some basis for this view because it was both held and defended in the medieval period and forcefully expostulated during the Reformation and Counter-Reformation. Spain was looked upon as the ideal model in this respect; it was seen as *the* "Catholic" nation. (Its influence, thus, on countries to the south of us was never favorably accepted by the establishment in the United States.) Such theories were hotly debated, especially in the last century, with the rise of democratic principles and with new experiments such as were found in the United States. It is also true that papal documents were ambiguous. They did not favor religious or democratic pluralism, because they would thus seem to approve of a religious relativism. The First Vatican Council tolerated a situation in which the Catholic religion was at least on an equal footing with all the others, more out of necessity than out of conviction.

But the condemnation of Americanism by Pope Leo XIII seemed like a victory for those who opposed the U.S. concept of separation of Church and state as a matter of principle. The integrists, so strong at that time, especially rejoiced. They saw this condemnation as a vindication of their position that everything—including the state—must become formally and explicitly Catholic before it could be good and "integral" or whole; everything, they stated, must be brought under the orbit of the Church. Such integrist views of the relationship between Church and state, we must admit, continued to exist in the Church, especially in France. One could cite, for example, the *Action française,* the writings and influence of Charles Maurras (1868–1952), the attempts to restore the monarchy, the political and religious ferments behind the Pétain regime, and the vehement opposition of such speakers as Archbishop Marcel Lefebvre during the debate on religious freedom at the Second Vatican Council. (It is difficult to explain the fact that Monsignor Lefebvre has such a large following here in the United States, when he stands for the very opposite of those principles upon which our nation is founded.) We would have to admit, too, that some of these views still remain as unreflected and uninformed notions by some integrist press and articles.

Without doubt, however, the turning point in the Church's thinking came with the *Declaration on Religious Liberty* in the Second Vatican Council. Perhaps one could say that the change in the thinking on Church/state relationships came about indirectly, that is, through its reflections on freedom of conscience and on religious liberty.

One could sum up the position of this document as follows: The basis for religious freedom is to be found in the very dignity of the human person. The content of that right is that the person in his or her pursuit for religious truth and its expression is to be protected from unjustified intrusion by the State or by others. This right can be exercised personally or corporately and should not be restricted unless it can be clearly shown that the form of external expression would be dangerous to the public order of society. In this search for religious truth the dictates of the human conscience must be followed. No one can be coerced to accept a religious truth; it must be the force of the truth itself which convinces.

In accepting this priority of values—religious liberty and freedom of conscience—the bishops knew that they were accepting then as normative for the future a pluralism of religious belief and expression in any given society. Indirectly the Church was putting a stamp of approval on the American system of consitutional government with its separation of Church and state; it abandoned all pretenses of wanting a "Catholic" state. (It is interesting that the Spanish bishops I know tell me that this declaration has been most important and useful to them in this post-Vatican II world.)

Although in this document the Church accepted the principle of separation of Church and state, it did not accept the separation of Church from society. Society is not coterminous with the state; it is broader in scope and includes all of those religious, social, economic, cultural, and moral organisms and organizations which act as intermediary or mediating structures between people and state. They form the fabric of society.

A further question then was discussed at length at the same Council: What should be the role of the Church in society? Those reflections form the content of that important document, the *Pastoral Constitution on the Church in the Modern World.* Here the Church does not see its activities exhausted by society's interests, aims, and concerns, since the Church has, in addition, its own proper religious and transcendent goals which flow from the Gospels and from its relationship to Christ and its duty to preach the Kingdom. On the other hand, the Church wants to be a participating member, together with all the other groups in society, without preference or favoritism, in forming the public consensus on given political and societal issues. The Church asks for the right to speak out as persons, community, and institution on the problems which affect society. It wants the freedom to participate in education, health concerns, and social services, and to discuss openly those issues which affect its members. In the light of Vatican II and the *Declaration on Religious Liberty,* it admits that consensus must be gained by informing consciences, not by coercion. It also wishes to do this ecumenically and with all people of good will. (I wish I could quote in full chapter IV of that *Pastoral Constitution on the Church in the Modern World,* where these mutual relationships between Church and world are spelled out. I leave that to the avid reader.)

The *Declaration on Religious Freedom* and the *Pastoral Constitution on the Church in the Modern World* were promulgated on December 7, 1965. It will be years before all of the implications of these far-reaching documents become a part of Catholic thinking and practices. But we must continue to make them our own and work out their practical implications.

No question, however, is as vexing to the Church in the United States as that of the correct interpretation of the separation of Church and state. From the beginning of our nation it has been the source of so much freedom for the Catholic Church, more than our European counterparts could ever have imagined. We only have to recall the many ways in current history in which the Church has been "co-opted" for political purposes and then was slow to respond to the menaces which were before it. The Church still suffers from criticism because it did not respond sooner and more clearly and forcefully to the Nazi menace and the totalitarian dictatorship of Mussolini. Separation of Church and state was not just a benefit to protect the secular order, but a real benefit to guard the prophetic mission of the Church in society.

We are rightly concerned today when that balance could be lost by wrong moves on the Church's part which could tie it into the party system or place it in a compromising political stance. (Some see the nuclear statement in this light.) We are rightly concerned, as well, about moves on the part of the state which might tend to curtail its liberty and freedom. (Some see the creation of ambassadorial relationships with the Holy See in this light.) It is thus the moment for the Church to articulate clearly and unambiguously where it is in this question and how it interprets that important concept of separation of Church and state.

One of the current fallacies of our day is the interpretation of this time-honored value to mean that political issues have no moral content and thus are outside the realm of religious consideration.

The first amendment to the Constitution makes it clear there will be no officially recognized state religion; there will be no interference in the internal workings of a Church, and freedom of religious expression is guaranteed. The first amendment does not define separation of Church and state as meaning that the Church exists somehow outside the common good of society and is not affected by the whole of society, nor that decisions made in the political sphere are outside moral considerations. Because political issues can and do contain varying degrees of moral consequences, the Church will always be reflecting on such issues in the light of its teaching and in the light of the Gospel message. Not to do so would be to renege on its duty and mission. The Church should reflect on those moral dimensions with courage but also with a certain humility because of their complexity and the fluid nature of any society. Being clergy or laity does not give anyone a kind of special knowledge that could lead to arrogance.

Some today would try to reduce morality to personal acts of the individual and deny that politics can be of a moral nature. In the present debate we must guard against this subtle assumption. What is for the common good has indeed a moral content. Today we do not reflect enough on the importance of the common good and the implication of acts and decisions which affect that common good as moral acts to be so judged.

As the Church—clergy and laity—reflects on the moral principles involved in important decisions which regard our community, state, nation, and world, it is impossible to avoid some application of those principles to real and concrete situations. Sometimes the application will be clear, sometimes vague. Sometimes the clarifications and "ifs" needed will make the application complicated and problematic. Sometimes the application will show many possibilities; other times only one course of action will seem to be open. At times the whole issue may be of minor importance. One of the most difficult moments of application comes when conflicting rights are involved and one must look at the aggregate of the whole and not just at a single issue. So many of the writings of Pope John Paul II help us in those circumstances with his insistence on the value of each individual person and the quality of that person's life as a primary value, to be sought before all others.

Although the degree of specificity may vary in each decision, it should not be assumed that the clergy has a monopoly on principles of morality and the lay people on their application. This is an unreal dichotomy. Both must struggle to enunciate the principles and to reflect on their application. For example, it would not have been fruitful or convincing if the clergy of Germany in the late 1930's and early 1940's had decided only to preach against racism and not to apply this to the Hitler regime. Or today it would be unrealistic to say that the Church should only talk of atheism and never apply it to specific regimes in communist countries.

In the political realm one can analyze, for its moral implications, a course of action which has already been determined. Here the clergy are no more nor less capable of discussing the issue than the laity, if all the information is available and if they have the technical knowledge and training necessary. The same could be said when different political options are open and being weighed according to their moral content. When the question is not one of moral content but of wisdom and political savvy, the Church should have no political stance. It is up to each citizen to weigh the evidence as it stands.

To many Catholics this whole area of the relationship between the political and their faith seems like a new and perhaps threatening argument. So many say that they dislike hearing the clergy preaching politics. I, too, would dislike having the clergy preach politics. But clergy must reflect on moral issues in the light of the Gospel if these issues are questions facing our community. No one would like to hear sermons which are always reflecting on political-moral issues to the exclusion of other matters as prayer, personal morality, and the virtues. No one would want the pulpit to become a political platform or an instrument of a political party. Slowly we will become more comfortable with these distinctions and begin to see the difference between that which is exclusively political and that which involves Gospel values.

There are two temptations which the Church must be aware of at this particular juncture of history. The Church must not permit its adversaries, nor its members, to force it to be quiet on serious moral national concerns. The Church must not enter political issues only when they involve its interest—such as tuition tax credits—and avoid other issues which do not greatly affect its inner life. To do so would be an easier course; the Church would receive less abuse and keep out of the public eye, but it would be selfish and lacking in prophetic courage. On the other hand, the Church must be on its guard against a second temptation, the seeking of power and the attempt to wield power in the political arena. Some who support the Church's stands are nevertheless a bit concerned at this moment that the Church may become power-hungry in the United States. The history of the Church in past ages indicates some basis for this fear. The separation of Church and state is one of those sacred blessings we have enjoyed and one which must be preserved. The Church only weakens itself if it seeks political power, as it can so easily become the pawn of forces which tend to compromise its teachings and force it to endless trade-offs. The Catholic Church in the United States today should repeatedly make it clear to all that it does not seek to create a political party nor to align itself with one. It should also make it clear that it does not aim to seek power—only to teach truth.

We have seen some try to destroy candidates on the basis of a single issue, and thus the question is asked: Will the Church tell people they cannot vote for a candidate who does not support their policy on nuclear deterrence? One would not put it that bluntly, but the question underneath it all is: Will the Church want to control the government? We are intelligent enough, it is hoped, and well enough informed from history to know that power corrupts. The Church must always reject power to be free. But that does not mean that the Church will not at times take unpopular stands for moral reasons and suffer the political consequences of such actions.

The Church sees its mission as one of preaching the Gospel message, of creating a community of love and healing, but also of working for a just and peaceful society. The belief it teaches must find its logical consequence in life and action. Faith is not only of the mind but also of the heart and hands and feet.

The Church Universal and Cultural Adaptations

The question of unity of faith in diversity of cultural expression is very much alive today. Most of the time our discussion centers on Africa or Asia where the question is rising for the first time with a certain seriousness. It would be wrong, however, to think it has been solved for the United States. Every attempt to face the relationship between the principles which were at the basis of the U.S. political experiment and how all of this related to the legitimate expression of faith in the United States met an *échec*. Thus the problem remains underground. Attempts to bring it out in the open, a typical American desire, are often met with accusations of disloyalty. The whole concept of loyal opposition has no Church context. At this moment the question seems more urgent.

In December 1981, Desmond O'Grady, an Australian journalist living in Rome, wrote an article for *Our Sunday Visitor* on how Rome views the Church in the United States. In it he readily admitted that in Rome "there is a feeling that the Atlantic has widened." One could say that from the U.S. side there are also signs of a widening gap. Perhaps it would be wise then to look at some of the historical roots of these perceptions to gain a better understanding of this stress point. We Americans are short on history; the Roman Curia has a long memory.

We must not forget that the Church in the United States started and grew during a time when Rome was fighting the last vestiges of Gallicanism—a movement which always challenged Roman authority and tended more and more toward a "French" Church. Then came the struggle against the Enlightenment and the Deistic philosophies which supported it. The anti-institutionalism involved in the new rationalism threatened the Church and made Rome very leery about the theological principles upon which the U.S. Constitution was founded. These principles were identified with the French Revolution and Freemasonry and were considered inimical to the Church and its structure. To the twenty-five thousand Catholics in the United States at the time of the Declaration of Independence they were, on the contrary, the source of new freedom and created the possibility of growth and expansion in a pluralistic society. When Bishop John Carroll wrote in 1784 that "America may give proof to the world that general and equal toleration, by providing a free climate for fair argument, is the most effectual method of bringing all denominations of Christianity into a unity of faith," the Roman Curia was aghast and saw the trend as most dangerous. These fears of the "American experiment" and the question of how much these concepts of the Enlightenment infiltrated Catholic thought in the United States led in 1899 to the condemnation of "Americanism" by Pope Leo XIII. This condemnation of Americanism was followed soon by a condemnation of Modernism by Pius X in 1907, and the two were inevitably connected in people's minds. As a young priest I had to take the oath against Modernism numerous times, and still today one finds the term being hurled against any proponent of a new idea.

To explain the results of these two condemnations on the Church and seminaries in the United States, I quote from James Hennesey, S.J. and his recent book, *American Catholics: A History of the Roman Catholic Community in the U.S.* (New York, 1981): "American Catholics had known an inchoate moment of native constructive theological thought.

They now slipped more or less peaceably into a half-century's theological hibernation" (p. 203). And: "The combination of Americanist and Modernist crises, and particularly the powerful integrist reaction which set in after 1907, effectively put an end for the next fifty years to further development of Catholic thought in authentic American dress" (p. 217).

In the light of this history one can see better why Rome in the middle of the last century would not name the archbishop of Baltimore the primate of the Church in the United States and why they would not permit the country to have uniform holy days of obligation in all the dioceses. Archbishop Francis Kenrick wrote in 1852 that Rome opposed this uniformity because "it tends to give a national character to the Church in the U.S.A." When the American bishops, after the First World War, formed the National Catholic Welfare Council, it was seen as a national Church structure and suppressed by Pius XI in 1922, only to be reinstated four months later with the proviso that it must be non-conciliar, non-legislative, and the name changed from "Council" to "Conference." It also explains so much of the controversy surrounding Vatican II's *Declaration on Religious Liberty*, where all of this history was played out again, our own Cardinal Albert Meyer being one of the staunch defenders of the American contribution. In our own day it explains why some of the changes in the Second Vatican Council found the Church here unprepared. When I did my studies in Rome after the Second World War, I had the privilege of hearing lectures whose ideas were to become those of the whole Church in Vatican II: Cyprian Vagaggini in theology and liturgy, Augustin Bea in Scripture and ecumenism, Athanasius Miller in Scripture, and so on. My classmates here in the United States were memorizing the old manuals of Tanqueray.

Some passages in documents of Vatican II—those on liturgy, the missions, the Church, revelation, and the role of bishops, for example—opened up again all of the old fears of Modernism and Americanism, especially in the United States. It is true that some of the false notions of the last century—rationalism, scientism, materialism, secularism, agnosticism—had never been put to rest. It is also true that Vatican II's concept of the people of God could so easily be mistaken for an approbation of democracy or the determination of truth by popular vote. Ecumenism could easily seem to be an approval of religious relativism. Liturgical adaptation to various cultures could easily lead again to nationalism, as could the formation of conferences of bishops. All of these fears have awakened a new wave of integrism in the United States and have found a ready ear in some Roman quarters, still looking with caution and ambivalence on the American Church in a pluralistic and democratic society.

When I returned from Rome in 1977, I read for the first time, however, in the integrist press (in *The Wanderer,* for example) of the formation of an "American Church" separated from Rome. In recent years the same press even put me up as the leader of such a movement! In all the time now that I have been back I have never been present when any group has ever discussed such an idea and I do not know any bishop, myself being number one, who would even be interested in discussing such a silly notion. But, unfortunately, such accusations, without evidence, create a continual atmosphere of fear and tend to put even more wedges of suspicion between an already cautious Curia and the Church in the United States.

And it is easy to understand why, at the meeting in Rome in January of 1983 between the American bishops involved in the debate on nuclear war and deterrence and

European bishops, Cardinal Ratzinger of the Congregation for the Doctrine of the Faith was concerned so much about the authority and power of a conference of bishops such as that of the United States to issue a statement of that sort.

More time should be spent discussing all of these historical events which affect the post-Vatican II Church in the United States in its relationship to Rome, but the above is sufficient to show how many are the unresolved tensions and how deep their roots that have made some observers agree with Desmond O'Grady that the Atlantic has been getting wider.

At the basis of much of the tension is the question of the teaching authority of a conference of bishops. The Revised Code of Canon Law states, "Bishops who are in communion with the head and members of the college, either individually or gathered together, whether in episcopal conferences or particular councils, although they do not have infallibility in teaching, are authentic teachers and masters of the faith for the Christians committed to their care." In itself this statement seems simple enough; but in practice the various levels of teaching authority in the Church are very complex and are the source of confusion and tension. Sometimes the Pope speaks infallibly (but rarely); at other times he teaches what the Church has universally taught but not always clearly defined as dogma; at times he articulates the held belief of the Church without stating for each point the weight to be placed on it.

Chapter 25 of *Lumen Gentium* of the Second Vatican Council speaks of this ordinary teaching authority and its recognizability: "This loyal submission of the will and intellect must be given, in a special way, to the authentic teaching authority of the Roman Pontiff, even when he does not speak *ex cathedra* in such wise, indeed that his supreme teaching authority be acknowledged with respect, and sincere assent be given to decisions made by him, conformably with his manifest mind and intention, which is made known principally either by the character of the documents in question, or by the frequency with which a certain doctrine is proposed, or by the manner in which the doctrine is formulated." This is a difficult text and, as one can see, demands on the part of the recipient of the teaching rather complicated judgments. In addition, we have various levels of papal documents, each one implying a different weight—encyclicals, *motu proprios,* apostolic letters, exhortations, speeches, homilies, etc. The Sacred Congregations in Rome also issue documents and decrees. What weight is to be attributed to each one of these? Often they state at the end that they were approved by the Pope in a papal audience on such and such a day. Does this mean that the Pope adds to the document the weight of his own personal teaching office? Does one Sacred Congregation, such as that of the Doctrine of the Faith, have more teaching authority than another? What about the weight of pronouncements of the secretary of state?

Such questions have been made more pressing by two new levels in the Church since Vatican II: What is the weight of documents produced by the Synod of Bishops? What is the weight of documents coming forth from conferences of bishops? This latter question poses a whole set of new questions. (I omit here the issue raised by the new pastoral, *The Challenge of Peace: God's Promise and Our Response.* Several times it states that the teaching of the principles of Catholic doctrine by the bishops has more weight than practical applications, almost as if there were a sliding scale of possibility of errancy as one progresses from the abstract to the concrete.)

As an example to show this complexity, I take a recent book by J. Brian Benestad, *The Pursuit of a Just Social Order:*

Policy Statements of the U.S. Catholic Bishops, 1966–80, published by the Ethics and Public Policy Center in Washington, D.C. (1982). In this lengthy analysis the author makes no differentiation of weight between documents voted on by the full assembly of bishops and statements of the officers of the conference, of staff members in their official capacity, or in lectures they may have given sometime or another. These distinctions are known to the author, as evidenced from an appendix to the book. Theologically viewed, his study is vitiated by this lack of differentiation. A document voted on by the full conference of bishops certainly has more weight than a speech made by a staff member! Moreover, he views only one segment of the bishops' activity—statements from one office; then he builds a theory around it. For example, he faults the bishops for not being concerned about evangelization and justice education and for separating those concerns from the pursuit of justice. He makes no reference to any of the documents of the Bishops' Committee on the Liturgy nor of the Bishops' Committee on Ecumenical Affairs, even though they have profound effects on the Church as evangelizer. Even the *ad hoc* Bishops' Committee on Evangelization is not mentioned nor the lengthy discussion on evangelization itself, whether it is best pursued on the national or local level. Also, no mention is made of *The National Catechetical Directory for Catholics in the United States, Sharing the Light of Faith* over which the bishops labored so assiduously. That document was prepared by the Committee on Education and a whole section is devoted to "Catechesis for Social Ministry." Reading his book was like going into the shoe section of a department store and then coming out upset because they did not sell shirts there. One must look at the whole.

I will admit, though, that all of this complexity has made the teaching authority of the Church more ambiguous. We receive papal teaching, as mentioned, in so many different forms; we receive documents of varying weight from Roman congregations, from the Synod of Bishops, from conferences of bishops, from individual bishops, from agencies within a diocese. Then we are told of the sliding scale from abstract to concrete.

All of this complexity may be doing harm, too, to the very teaching mission of the Church. Two errors of approach are possible. One would be to disregard all such distinctions and accept everything—at least from the Papal and Roman Congregations—rather fundamentalistically, that is, without any distinctions. Thus, the prohibition against altar girls has the same weight as the teaching on abortion. The other extreme would be to relativize everything, as if it all were on the same level, depending on whether one agreed or not. Many fall into this error; they reject the teaching on abortion as easily as if it were the prohibition against altar girls. Both of these extremes are wrong and not true to Catholic tradition. Theologians, by profession, must continue to sort out these "weights" and delve into the richness of the process. But what about us less fortunate? Somehow we all more or less learned as kids when dad really meant no and when we could still coax a bit; we more or less learned when something was serious and when it was trivial. Perhaps in the Church we functioned a bit, too, by this instinct. Nevertheless, at this juncture of history we all might have to become a bit more discriminating and theologically a bit more sophisticated in this whole process of how Popes and bishops teach.

In addition to the problem of confusion which arises when several conferences of bishops take up and deal with the same theme—for example, the question of possession of nuclear weapons and deterrences—and seem to come up with different answers, there is the problem of understanding issues which are urgent and pressing in one culture but seemingly unimportant, almost not comprehensible, in others. Sometimes we in the United States feel that way about the whole question of liberation theology and the relationship it seems to make between freedom from sin (salvation) and freedom from economic or military oppression (liberation). We seem baffled before the whole question of the rise of socialism in third world nations.

In our American culture socialism is a bad word (even, I see, here in Milwaukee which had experienced socialist mayors for many years). On March 4, 1979, as accurately reported the next day by *The Milwaukee Journal,* I used the phrase in a talk at UW-M, entitled "Marx and the Bible in Latin America." In that conference I quoted a document produced by the bishops of Latin America gathered at Medellín, Colombia (1968) in which they rejected both "the system of liberal capitalism and the temptation of the Marxist system" as militating against the dignity of the human person. They also lamented the fact that Latin America found itself "caught between these two options" and remained dependent on one or the other of the centers of power which controlled its economy. It was in this context that I raised in a favorable light the examination in South America of a possible Christian socialism. (As one can see, the context was limited to that section of the world. I would not be so unrealistic as to assume that such an idea would be applicable to our own society, a society which is not very "Christian" indeed.)

Socialism is a very ambivalent term, as any dictionary will point out. Christian socialism is no different. It is sometimes used, especially in its European origins, to mean a democratic form of government that centralized much of the economic control and planning in the elected government; its ideals generally centered around a balancing of the concerns of the individuals with the common good. Most Americans equate the word "socialism" with Marxist collectivism, in which case "Christian socialism" becomes a contradiction in terms. Often in Europe the socialist party had no historical roots in Marxism (as in Germany); at other times it was a break-off from the communist party (as in Italy). From the end of the last century to more recent times the Catholic Church has usually shunned any kind of endorsement of socialist tendencies because of the affinity with Marxism and because of the Church's strong defense of private property against those who were confiscating the Church's property.

The discussion of a new and Christian approach to socialism came as a result of the apostolic letter of Pope Paul VI in 1971, two years after the Medellín conference of Latin American bishops cited above. In that letter, called *Octogesima Adveniens,* the Pope stated that there was a need for Christians to discern carefully the degree of commitment possible to socialism that would safeguard "the values, especially those of liberty, responsibility and openness to the spiritual, which guarantee the integral development of the human person." No easy task, to be sure!

In the years which followed many such attempts were made in Catholic countries; of special interest was the movement in Chile in 1972–73 and the statement by the French hierarchy on May 1, 1972. Both groups used the term Christian socialism because they felt that their countries were rooted historically in Christian values, and the Gospel should thus be at the basis of any social reform. Both of these were attempts to avoid collectivism as well as statism, probably an easier danger to avoid in theory than in practice. Since then many South American nations have toyed with these concepts and will continue to do so. Generally they avoid the term "Christian socialism" to avoid confusion. Naturally, it is pointed out at once to such advocates that in practice the step to communism is an easy and tempting one, with the inevitable loss of freedom. The answer one receives, often with bitterness, is that we in the United States, to maintain our own security and freedoms, permit theirs to be suppressed by right-wing military dictatorships. The risk is ours, not theirs, they will say; they have nothing to lose. Wrongly or rightly, these accusations are made more often than we would like to hear. We usually respond with the oft-repeated criterion that our free-market system has brought capitalist countries a higher standard of living with higher benefits than have ever been experienced in history before. This is undoubtedly true; no one could deny the point. (Having visited communist countries in the East bloc so many times in my life, I would have to say, although one sees no real misery, that they are uniformly drab and poor, without taking into account the deprivation of human rights that occurs there.)

It is fair enough to judge an economic system by economic standards, but that is not a sufficient criterion for judging a *society.* Here I think that the recent writings and speeches of Pope John Paul II (no lover of capitalism or communism) are helpful. His criterion is always that of how well the system protects and promotes the dignity of each human person. He said in Philadelphia on October 3, 1979: "Human-Christian values triumph by subjecting political and economic considerations to human dignity, by making them serve the cause of man—every person created by God, every brother and sister redeemed by Christ." He had expressed the same concept earlier at Puebla in Mexico, January 28, 1979: "This complete truth about the human being constitutes the foundation of the Church's social teaching and the basis also of true liberation. In the light of this truth man is not a being subjected to economic or political processes; these processes are, instead, directed to man and are subjected to him." Thus, I do not fault the Central and South American countries for looking for a way out, usually in Christian socialism, where the integrity of their nations and the values of a society based on the equality and the dignity of each member can be maintained. If they fail, it should come from their own mismanagement and inner power struggles and not from outside pressures.

Pope Paul gave us a tough row to hoe when he said in that same document, *Octogesima Adveniens,* that the Church cannot align itself with any particular political party, but the Church also cannot remain neutral insofar as injustice is concerned. In 1979, ten years after the Latin American bishops had met in Medellín, Colombia, they met again in Puebla, Mexico. As previously, they were harsh in their treatment of both capitalism and Marxism, without pointing out to their priests and people a third option. However, they state the following as their positive pastoral thrust: " . . . a bold Christian profession and an effective promotion of human dignity and its divine foundations. And this is to be done specifically among those who are most in need of it— either because they despise human dignity or, even more importantly, because they suffer from this scorn and are seeking, however gropingly, for the freedom of the children of God and the coming of the new human being in Jesus Christ." This is reiterated at the end of the document: "We must create in the people of Latin America a sound moral conscience, a critical-minded evangelical sense vis-à-vis reality, a communitarian spirit, and a social commitment. All this will allow for free, responsible participation, in a spirit of fraternal communion and dialogue, aimed at the construction of a new society that is truly human and suffused with evangelical values."

Is this a new Christian socialism? How can one change it and call it a new Christian capitalism? Is it that by balancing the rugged individualism with a new emphasis on the common good? What relationship exists outside our own nation between capitalism and military and totalitarian dictatorships? These questions are raised to show the breadth of the economic and political questions which the Church must be involved in as we approach the year 2000. Political and economic issues determine the kind of society we and the rest of the world will live in and be a part of. No wonder they are now coming forth as crucial for the Church. For us in the United States they have great urgency because of our national leadership. We are a Church which is an integral part of a nation that will help determine the political and economic future of many other nations; our responsibility in this area is thus unique and pressing.

The Church of the Year 2000

Earlier I mentioned areas which will be determining the agenda of the universal Church until the year 2000. It is difficult to select only a few as being more urgent or important than others. Certainly, for example, ecumenism is one such area. On the other hand, one feels that a certain sure beginning has been made since the Second Vatican Council, and that although there will be ups and downs and stagnant periods, the thrust is now too much a part of our existence for any ultimate retrenchment to take place. The economic issues just mentioned are also areas where the Church has a consistent social teaching since *Rerum Novarum* of Pope Leo XIII of 1891 and where a good basis has been laid. The same can now be said of the nuclear threat which hangs over us all. Peace has become a priority and we will continue to probe the teaching already given.

The two specific areas I want to mention here which will be on the agenda of the Church till the year 2000 are the role of women and all those questions related to human sexuality. Elsewhere I touched on this first issue. The Church cannot credit itself for being or having been a leader in reassessing the role of women; that movment began outside the Church and, thanks to so many sisters and courageous laywomen, is beginning to affect in a positive fashion the role of women in the Church as well. There is rightfully much fear and hesitation in this area because of some of the violence of the rhetoric and because extreme positions often are not carefully examined—positions which most true feminists do not hold and which cause new injustices to the other half of the world and Church.

At one time the role of women was considered just "an American issue"; today it is seen as a concern of the universal Church. It is more than just the issue of altar girls or ordination of women. It enters every aspect of Church life and structure. And it will not just go away and be forgotten. I realize that the ramifications of this issue are so large that the universal Church has difficulty dealing with it and seeking out some kind of logical and cohesive way of airing it so that unity is not harmed. The recent history of other Churches is reason enough for caution! On the other hand, excessively long delays with no signs of breakthroughs cause many to be bitter and angry and to leave the Church. We are now feeling such repercussions in the United States. From the suffering and confusing emotional reactions which one has to be a part of these days as this issue continues to challenge our socio-political and religious structures, one hopes that a purification will result which will eventually strengthen the Church and make it freer.

The other set of questions which will be a constant part of the agenda till 2000 and beyond involves human sexuality. I am not one for "changing the rules" at this moment, but I am one for continual study of the psychological and sociological nature of the human person. I regret very much that the Church sometimes gives the impression it has a low esteem for these human sciences. It may be true that psychology and sociology are still in their infancy when compared to physics and chemistry, but they have already made a profound contribution to our knowledge of the human person and will continue to do so. Human sexuality is one of those areas where the Church will have to keep itself abreast of research and continue to re-evaluate its stands in the light of new findings. It is not easy to do so since people call out constantly for guidance and help. Wisdom remains on the side of the traditional moral teaching—it has been tried for so long and proven helpful—until a more sure scientific basis results. I take two examples of this need for prudence and where knowledge is still rudimentary. Masturbation and homosexuality are two such cases where scientific knowledge is still very deficient. In the latter case, scientists still are much divided on the origins and nature of homosexual orientation. One year a book comes out to prove it is acquired, the next year another book with a new set of research data proves the opposite!

To many the Church may seem intransigent before the opinion polls on artificial birth-control, but scientific research may well prove the wisdom of its caution since the time of Pope Paul VI to Pope John Paul II. One could easily say that the facts are not all in yet. In spite of the difficulties of working in an area which is still not totally understood—and our knowledge of the human person is yet in its infancy—there is a certain need for wisdom and calm, as well as caution, lest each new theory become the basis of new moral rules that must be discarded with next year's theory.

Perhaps only a closer and more trusting relationship between Church and scientists will avoid such pitfalls.

There are undoubtedly other areas not touched on here which seem urgent and where more trust among the members of the Church is needed. Perhaps we do not have as yet in the Church those forums where divergent opinions can be voiced without fear of reprisals. Structures such as parish councils, diocesan pastoral councils, and the like often tend to be more lay forums for administrative detail than for vision-sharing of pastoral and theological perspectives.

But the ultimate aim of "Church" is fellowship, or communion, and not the victory of an ideology. All, regardless of what "faction" each adheres to, must strive and struggle toward the same goal of union. The same Gospel, the same tradition, the same Spirit bind all. No one wins and no one loses; but all seek to discern what God wants of the Church today. His Spirit blows where it will, and thus discerning is more important than debate and media agitation. Discernment takes place as much in the quietude of prayer and reflection as in rhetoric and fine words. Since the aim or scope of the Church is also to continue Jesus' mission of salvation on earth and since the Church's aims are not the same as those of any political society, its structure and functioning must be different. Transposing to it a U.S. democratic structure would make no sense. Right and wrong, Gospel values, and promptings of the Spirit are not determined by voting or majority rule.

What the Church needs, thus, is not any structures which will politicize it, but ways of permitting all the different gifts of all the faithful to find their expression, so that all contribute to their wisdom and insight—from theologian and university professor to homemaker. The Spirit blows where it will. We need structures which help us listen to the fine tuning of the Gospel message and do not need scramblers which only deafen us and distort the message.